SUSIE BRIGHT'S SEXUAL REALITY:

A Virtual Sex World Reader

Published in the United States by Cleis Press Inc., P.O. Box 8933, Pittsburgh, Pennsylvania 15221, and P.O. Box 14684, San Francisco, California 94114.

Printed in the United States.
Cover design: Ellen Toomey
Cover photo: Phyllis Christopher
Typesetting: CaliCo Graphics
Logo art: Juana Alicia

Library of Congress Cataloging-in-Publication Data

Bright, Susie. 1958-
   [Sexual reality]
   Susie Bright's sexual reality : a virtual sex world reader. — 1st ed.
      p.   cm.
   ISBN 0-939416-58-1 (cloth) : $24.95. — ISBN 0-939416-59-X (pbk.) : $9.95
   1. Sex customs — United States.   2. Lesbians — United States —
Sexual behavior.   I. Title.
HQ18.U5B75   1992
306.7'0973 — dc20   92-13740
                                             CIP

First Edition.
10 9 8 7 6 5 4 3 2 1

Grateful acknowledgment is made to *Penthouse Forum* for permission to reprint "Story of O Birthday Party."

SUSIE BRIGHT'S SEXUAL REALITY:

A
Virtual Sex World
Reader

CLEIS
PRESS

ACKNOWLEDGMENTS

This Virtual Sex World Reader was written in world record time with the support and assistance of Lisa Palac, Jon Bailiff, Honey Lee Cottrell, Rebecca Hall, Bill Tonelli, my good friends in Puéchabon, my publishers Felice Newman and Frédérique Delacoste, and of course, those Good Vibrations gals. Thank you.

Versions and portions of these stories first appeared in *Elle*, *Forum*, *Esquire*, *NYQ*, *The Advocate*, *Hustler Erotic Video* and *Image*. Thank you to the publishers of these magazines and my editors there: Jenny Plath, Liz McKenna and Don Myrus, Bill Tonelli, Maer Roshan, Doug Brantley, Scott Mallory and David Talbot.

This book is for my father.

ABOUT THE AUTHOR

S usie Bright is the author of *Susie Sexpert's Lesbian Sex World* (Cleis Press, 1990). She edited *Herotica* (Down There Press) and *Herotica II* (Plume Books) and is a former editor of *On Our Backs*, the magazine for the "adventurous" lesbian. Her lectures, video presentations and safe sex demos pack theaters in the United States, Canada and Europe. Perhaps the first lesbian sex guru to grace the pages of *Rolling Stone*, Susie Bright was named Reason #23 among *Minneapolis Weekly's* "62 Reasons to Love America." She has one daughter, Aretha, who is two years old.

CONTENTS

9   Introduction

17   Story of O Birthday Party

27   Shiny Plastic Dildos Holding Hands

37   Rape Scenes

45   Strip Tea

55   A Good Butch Is Hard to Find:
Masculinity in the Nineties

60   The Virtual Orgasm

71   Undressing Camille

87   Sex and The Single Pest

93   Men Who Love Lesbians
(Who Don't Care for Them Too Much)

99   Egg Sex

109   When No Means I Didn't Know It
Would Be Like This

118   Lynnie Is the Queerest Thing on This Street

125   Lynnie and the Kamikaze Heart

133   Lesbians, Lies, Secrets and Silence
        (Or What Goes Around Comes Around)

140   I Got This Way From Kissing Donahue

150   BlindSexual

INTRODUCTION TO SEXUAL REALITY

Every night before I go to bed, I do a little *Star Trek* dance. Actually it's every night when my toddler goes to bed that this space age tribal stomp begins. But these days, our bedtime hour is practically the same.

The *Star Trek* dance goes along with the *Star Trek: The Next Generation* music, which is very grand and pompous. We fly around the room, arms outstretched, one moment an eagle, the next a rocket ship. Then there are the ballerina moves, the coronation postures, and last but not least, spinning like a top.

My imagination is very uninhibited around my daughter, because she's so good at pretending that everything we make up is REAL. Fantasies are the stuff of pure joy. We can do anything and be anybody we want, and when it all gets too exciting, we collapse in a heap on the floor. Game over.

Perhaps toddlers should be the cerebral executives in charge of the new technology that has promised to revolutionize our imaginations. When I first heard the expression "virtual reality," or even the buzzword "virtual" all by itself, I had no idea what it meant. I was given an assignment last spring by *Elle* magazine to find out how new media/computer technology was going to affect our sex lives, and I spent the first week of my research going, "I don't get it."

But once I got past the jargon and saw examples of virtual technology—a type of 3-D make-your-own television experience—I fell in love not with the technology per se, but with the consciousness it provokes. Creating an experience that seems as if it were real, so accurate in all its details, is a testament to the power of make-believe. The very concept of "virtuality" proves how crucial our imagination is, how subversive and inexplicable our fantasy lives truly are.

You don't have to wait for any equipment to have a virtual experience. You've already had it. Every time you close your eyes and touch yourself, the mind pirouettes, and every sort of feeling floods your body. You bring yourself to orgasm not with a greased hand or a vibrator, or because someone has applied the perfect pressure to your clit, but because your mind takes you there. It pins you to the ground of your naughtiest visions and only releases you when the tension explodes. Fantasy is the ultimate virtual experience because it feels *so real* and requires no accessories.

This collection of essays is not about computer visions. Instead, I have a lot to say about politics, erotics, and the human sexual condition. At one point, I wanted to call this volume *Men, Women, Children and Lesbians.* I figured that would cover all my current special interests. But I have been captivated by the idea of "virtual reality," by the recognition that our fantasies and fears—especially the sexual ones—are more real than the "real" forces we have reckoned with historically. I figure the virtual revolution is just a breath away from smashing our institutional state of mind.

The battle over what The Government will or won't let you do with your body has been the dominant culture clash of my generation. Last night, I saw some old footage of Alabama governor George Wallace sparring with a protester during his 1968 presidential run. He delighted his faithful audience by telling a demonstrator to "go see a barber; a barber could help you out a lot." Twenty-five years later, presidential candidate Pat Buchanan is doing TV spots showing shirtless men in leather pants dancing at a San

Francisco Street Fair—a real horror in Buchanan's book—
but you can't say those boys aren't clean-shaven and well-
groomed. Both scenes attacked sexuality—men accusing
other men of not being "real men." Meanwhile, the war
over who controls women's bodies and sexuality is even
more paternalistic, which shows what being called the
"weaker sex" will do to you.

Censorship, the modern code word for the repression of
sexual beliefs and practices, made history early in this
decade. Artists whose works violated sexual taboo—
whether Mapplethorpe's nudes, 2 Live Crew's lyrics or
Karen Finley's incantations—were attacked by an unusual combination of right-wingers and liberals. Right-
wingers wanted to shoot the rebels, while liberals just
wanted to stick a big label on their products: *Warning—Sex
Is Dangerous.*

Those who try to stamp out, criminalize and vilify forms
of sexuality that offend them are also the first to fall under
the virtual microscope that reveals their hypocrisy. Careful
not to trip on your robes, Judges—both federal, or worse
yet, self-appointed. Prudes and patriarchs all have sexual
thoughts which must undoubtedly trouble and betray
them, often making fools of their public postures. Hypo-
crites don't want to see their own private thoughts produced as commercial pornography, or rapped on albums,
or hanging in galleries. But if they can't stop themselves
from thinking about sex, how can they really stop anybody
else? They use the law to erode basic freedoms.

Censors have turned certain States of the Union into
blindfolded territories, but they can't stop the little minds
from fantasizing behind the blinders. You may find it rough
to buy a copy of *Susie Sexpert's Lesbian Sex World* in
Oklahoma, but you sure can find a lot of lesbians, a lot of
sex, and a world of taboo activities circulating throughout
the Sooner state. Go ahead, Jesse Helms, shred the Bill
of Rights into sweater lint, but we've got something in this

country—call it a virtual right to the pursuit of happiness—that cannot be removed, except perhaps by lobotomy. (Oh Virtual God, I hope I haven't given him another idea).

Susie Sexpert's Lesbian Sex World, my collection of essays on seven years of observing lesbian sex, culture and community politics, came out in 1990. It assaulted the traditional ways in which lesbians are regarded: as either lost girls or imitation men. It also challenged the lesbian feminist community to take up its self-interest in sexual liberation—or to get the hell out of the way.

Some dykes found it a perfect how-to manual, and I had several offers from women who wanted to add their heartfelt recommendations to the cover: "This really works!" or "Yes, now you too can slide your palm into your lover's vagina without special attachments!" I was happy to have demystified how women make love with each other—how women get off, period. But I knew that the sexual delight I heard from women readers was at least as much about their gathering confidence and courage as it was about mistressing some new technique.

I also got many letters from and introductions to non-lesbians—men and women—who blushingly presented themselves as admirers of my book. "I know it wasn't written for me," they said, "but I got so much out of it; it's so revealing." One guy said I should re-issue it under the new title: *Secrets of Women's Sexuality Uncovered by Genuine Lesbian*, but I told him *that* vision is already sewn up by the same guy who wrote *How To Pick Up Girls*. True enough, *Susie Sexpert's Lesbian Sex World* does share some of the under-publicized details of lesbian life, but I think the book spoke to varied audiences because a woman talking frankly about sex is good to find. Or maybe the details of lesbian life are less unique than I thought. The empathy I felt for my readers expanded as "my crowd" got more crowded.

Introduction

I got to know my audience during a book tour I did for *Susie Sexpert's Lesbian Sex World* in the fall of 1990. I had a new book and a new baby, Aretha. I employed my friend Rupa to be my nanny during a two-month tour of fifteen cities across the United States and Canada. Rupa was just back from a year in India, her hair dark purple and rings on every finger and toe. (Rupa is the same spirit with a bouffant who took me on the six-hour bus ride to see k.d. lang for the first time in a Tahoe casino—one of my favorite stories from *Sex World*.)

Our trip took us across the Canadian border. Remember that Canada defines obscenity as "what is degrading to women." What priceless objectivity! This definition springs from the most paternalistic opinions delivered by a high court in this century. Since the Canadian government is expert in degrading women, I guess the Canadian courts have their hands full of legitimate complaints.

My entry into Toronto was certainly an obscene joke by these standards. Every single finger of every single rubber glove that I had packed in my safe sex kit was examined, the white talcum power spilling out on the officer's desk like a scene from a *Saturday Night Live* skit. They questioned my identity as the mother of my child. Since nobody had warned me that birth certificates were required to enter Canada, the only thing I could do to prove I was Aretha's mom was to unleash my jaguar mother-rage. Any idiot customs official could see I would easily blow their fucking checkpoint into a million pieces.

Later in my tour, I crossed into Canada again, this time at Montreal, where there didn't seem to be a customs officer in the entire airport. I just walked out into the sunshine; a beautiful French-speaking woman escorted me to her car, and I proceeded to have the time of my life. Montreal was the only place on my trip where women asked me to autograph their breasts.

My memories of the book tour are all like this: from the

degrading to the sublime. In Northampton, Massachusetts, a police escort advised me not to eat out for fear of an anti-porn sniper attack. I was so angry and tearful—I didn't want to die for lesbian porn in western Massachusetts. Only in a place like Northampton would I need police protection and then be asked to speak in a CHAPEL. My rule of thumb: the more religious, puritanical or fundamentalist the territory, the kinkier it gets.

In Dallas, I was invited by a lesbian social group to speak at a lakeside country club, following a leather and fur fashion show. When one of the models dropped her full-length fox to the floor, revealing white lace lingerie, I whispered to my host, "If this was San Francisco, you would be burned at the stake by animal rights activists."

I think she misunderstood me. "Nobody is that militant here," she said. "Everyone in this room is in the closet."

My babysitter that night at the lake was a young man in leather chaps, vest and cap, who crooned to Aretha all night long. I asked my hostess why he was so instantly devoted to her. "He just had a baby three months ago," she said. "But his wife's in the service, and she and the baby are in South Carolina right now. He never knows when he's going to see that baby next."

"His *wife*?" I asked. I had to be reminded again, a little less gently, that many dykes and fags marry each other in Texas. And this young man was one proud father, his eyes shining as brilliantly as his polished chaps when he showed me his son's photo. I wonder how many of the leathermen Pat Buchanan televised dancing in the street are fathers, too.

So many people ask me, usually with a little apprehension in their voices, how I'm managing with Aretha, being a single mom. Do I have co-parents? Is the father involved? What will I tell her about my scandalous occupation when she's a little older?

I have provided some context and answers to all those

questions in the following chapters. But the big answer is this: I am just like all the other families in America who are neither nuclear nor tribal, who are creating a family life not seen on television, but a very, very real one. I rarely feel isolated or strange, because I've met too many people who make my circumstances look like those of a perfect square.

The most unusual aspect of my life isn't being a single mother or a radical sex activist. It's being a writer. I recently spoke on a panel where a fellow speaker railed against academics and artists who think they can change the world by sending out finely-crafted communiqués from their tower windows.

I'm not an academic, but I have been an artist who sat alone in my room for long periods of time. I have also been on the ground protesting, before a judge who called me "a menace to society," and on the phone talking quietly to strangers who I've tried to seduce into action as passionately as I would a lover. In between those times, I often read. My favorite books, the passages I go over and over again, inspire me completely, as music does, as does the way a certain dancer, a stripper, who uncoils her soul for me on stage.

If others didn't write such words to move me, I don't know if I would move. The best result of my work has been to be a muse, to inspire others to take a chance. I care about my craft; I want to communicate, and I have the confidence of a whore (with a heart of gold, naturally), to believe that words can change the world.

When I was sixteen, I read Victor Serge's *Memoirs of a Revolutionary.* I open it now and see that I underlined his ending:

"The future seems to me to be full of possibilities greater than any we have glimpsed throughout the past. May the passion, the experience, and even the faults of my fighting generation have some small power, to illuminate the way forward!"

And so here is my little illumination. Open your mind, virtually, spread your lips, literally, and to my every premeditated, lubricated intention: ENGAGE.

Susie Bright
San Francisco, March 1992

STORY OF O
BIRTHDAY PARTY

". . . a happy prisoner upon whom everything
was imposed and from whom nothing was asked."
—The Story of O

I had big plans for my thirtieth birthday party. Inspired by *Lifestyles of the Rich and Famous*, I planned to spoof the career expectations of the entire thirty-something generation by having a Filthy Rich and Wretchedly Famous Blowout where, diamond tiara on my head, I would preside over my royal Coming Of Age.

But my plans were changed for me. I never got close to a diamond tiara. In fact, I wore very little at all.

Two days before my birthday, my lover, Honey Lee, asked me if we could have the day all to ourselves. She had a little surprise. Surprises aren't Honey's forte, but I thought that after six years together I'd allow her attempt at unpredictability.

"Okay, I'd love to spend the day with you. Just tell me what to wear," I said. That turned out to be the key that pried open her secret.

"Nothing, nothing at all," she answered. "All you have to do is wake up in the morning and be ready for anything."

March 25th. I woke up, put on my furry purple bathrobe and set the kettle on to boil. I wasn't jumping to any conclusions. Honey Lee didn't seem to be in any particular hurry. "You're having some guests over at ten o'clock," she said.

I sipped my tea and imagined the possibilities. Two weeks

17

ago, I had been putting away Honey's bags and discovered a new paperback copy of *The Story of O*. Honey Lee credited Pauline Réage's classic S/M novel with every hot sexual fantasy ever to enter her head, but she was all sexy dreams and no action. Honey had never tied me up, slapped me, or spanked me. She said the real thing made her sick to her stomach. Was she about to turn it all around for my third decade?

I heard heavy steps approaching the front door. And who of our women friends was so big that she bumped her head on the ceiling?

It was no lesbian. It was a six-foot-tall man, with a head as bald as Yul Brynner's and an enormous wooden table in his arms.

"This is your masseur, Patrick," Honey Lee announced. "He'll be with you for the next two hours. I'll be back when he's finished."

I was speechless that she was leaving me alone with a giant. Patrick set up his massage table and covered it with a flannel sheet. I slipped out of my robe and thought, "Well, here we go." If Honey Lee was preparing me for something, I'd need every minute of a two-hour massage.

The masseur handled every corner of me, every pinch of flesh. He washed my feet and stroked my hair and pulled and kneaded me into a floating fog. When Honey returned, my face was as soft as a baby's and I could only mumble my thanks. She brought me a cup of tea and the doorbell rang again.

"Your dresser is here."

In walked a blond, curly-haired angel. It was my friend Debi, who works as a stripper and was dressed in one of her most outrageous costumes: white satin underwear and pearls, all covered by a sheer crinoline veil. But the clothes she had brought for me were even more spectacular.

First, she cinched my waist with a tight leather corset until I looked like an hourglass. She had me slip on black silk stockings. She rouged my nipples. Honey Lee brought out a black satin and gauze gown that exposed my breasts but covered my hips and legs. The lace tops of my stockings barely peeked out over the thigh-high leather stiletto boots she handed me. Debi crimped my hair and applied the same lipstick to my lips that she'd touched on my breasts. Such a beauty. By the time she was done with me, I could not make any coy remarks about my physical flaws. When I looked in the mirror, I saw Mistress Venus.

Honey packed up some parcels for the car. "I can't go out like this!" I protested. But Debi had already thought of that. She folded me into me her black patent leather trench coat. Now I was a sex slave with an Emma Peel wrapper.

Debi kissed me and gave me some last fairy godmother words of advice. "You won't be able to talk from now on," she said. "Anything you want to say to Honey Lee or me, you should say now."

I don't know what it was, but I burst into tears. "I love you so much. . . and I'm a little worried about what you have planned for me . . . I don't know if I can be quiet," I admitted.

Honey took my face in her hands. "Parts of today might be hard for you, Susie, but I don't think you'll regret it. Do you trust me?"

I nodded, but my heart did a flip-flop. I always fantasize about submission, but in real life, I am a control fanatic. I hated her for putting me to the test like this, and I couldn't believe the lengths she'd gone to prepare for it.

For all my fears of not being able to button my lip, I suddenly didn't feel like saying a word. Honey escorted me to the car. Debi, still in her bra and G-string, sped away in her Saab.

Honey Lee and I don't have many separate friends or secrets, and I know my way around the city better than she does. So when we drove for a half an hour only to end up in one of the worst neighborhoods in town, I was sure that she'd gotten us lost, the one torture I cannot abide. I was about to break my vow of silence and tell her to move aside, when she pulled into a parking space. "This is it!" she grinned.

Fabulous. Was I supposed to pirouette to the corner and let the gang bang begin? But Honey steered me towards the creaky stairs of the Victorian flat in front of us. We were buzzed in and she sent me ahead, up three flights of stairs.

The door at the end of the hall came ajar and my mouth opened as wide as the sky. Greeting us was a fully uniformed member of the San Francisco Police Department. She was a woman cop I recognized from the neighborhood I work in, someone to whom I'd never said more than "have a nice day." Honey and she shook hands like old friends.

"Kelly, how are you?" Honey started.

"I'm just on my way to work. All I have to do is polish my boots."

"What a coincidence," Honey said. They were both speaking like marionettes. "I just happen to have a boot polishing kit with me, and I think Susie would love to give you a nice shine."

I broke my quiet spell. "I don't remember how to shine shoes."

Honey snorted. "Shame on you. We'll give a you a little review."

Honey Lee handed me a shoeshine box with all the equipment. In the corner was a Post-it note reading, "I will be back for you. Do your very best. Love, René."

In *The Story of O*, René is the lover who requires O to submit to other men in order to prove her love and obedience to him. My premonition was coming true.

Kelly took me into her bedroom. She had a couple of guests visiting, a young man and woman who looked me over thoroughly and followed us to the doorway. "Can we watch?"

Kelly gave them the nod. I got out the black polish and tried to remember when the spitting part was supposed to be performed. She was very patient. In fact, for a police officer, I'd gotten a real pussycat. She saw how I kept eyeing her gun belt, and when I had polished her thick work boots as brilliantly as I could, she pulled me to my feet and asked, "You wanna try on my belt?"

She emptied the bullets out of her revolver and showed me where she stored her ammunition, her nightstick, cuffs and flashlight. She slipped the whole contraption around my hips. It must have weighed thirty pounds.

"How can you chase bad guys like this?" I was breaking the no-talking rule again, but Honey Lee wasn't around to keep discipline.

"I'm not interested in dying," she said. She preferred to sweat it out in a heavy bulletproof vest every shift.

"Honey Lee is going to be back before you know it," I said, pulling my original costume together. "You'd better tell her I didn't say a word."

Kelly handed me over with a high recommendation and no squealing. Honey drove us over the hills into yuppie heaven.

"The hardest part is coming up," she said. "Maybe harder for me than for you." She was headed for our friend Coral's apartment.

Coral is what I would call a gourmet sadomasochist. Her home is decorated and constructed for sex play. Her collection of sex toys, particularly whips, is Smithsonian caliber. Honey and I love to talk about sex, pain and pleasure with Coral, but we are intellectual companions, never participants. I wondered what kind of scene Coral could concoct with me, for if I was to be like O, then Coral would have to perform as a sadist, and I knew that would be a switch.

I should have guessed that Coral could dish out the pain/pleasure she loves to receive. She let us into the bottom floor of her penthouse with more authority and pure wickedness than I'd ever seen in her before.

"Of course, this is out of the ordinary for me," she said. "But I love to make exceptions for the very young and the very pretty."

She and Honey took me up to the master bedroom and told me to stand against the window while they talked about what to do with me. I felt a little rebellious.

"Look Coral, why don't I just turn you over and give you a good spanking. I should slap both of you for humiliating me like this."

They couldn't believe my cheek. "That's ten extra strokes right there," Honey said.

"Make that with the cane," Coral added.

"A cane! But I've never even been hit with so much as a feather duster!" I said. Coral's eyes got terribly bright all of a sudden. Oh yes, I was a virgin for her, a virgin bottom. The two of them instructed me to take my clothes off, one piece at a time, and pose for them in a completely exploitative way. I bent over in my leather boots and fingered the stretch between my ass and my cunt. I ran the pearls between my legs. I insulted them gamely. "Enjoy yourselves now, you little shits, because I'm going to turn the tables twice as hard when this is over!" Finally I had nothing left on but my stockings, the corset and my mother's rhinestone necklace. Coral invited me to approach her as she pulled a small red and black leather whip from her hip pocket. "I'm going to hand you the handle, and if you return it to me, it means you accept my authority."

I took my sweet time returning it to her. There is no one on earth I would let whip me except Coral. I trust her sensitivity and expertise, but I didn't know how I would react to the pain.

Honey Lee knew what was on my mind. "Do it for me, Susie," she said, and kissed my lips and hair. Then she put on her jacket. I started crying.

"You mean you aren't going to stay?" I sobbed.

"No, but I'll be close by," she promised.

I could tell it was harder for her to leave this time, and I didn't understand why.

Coral stretched me out belly down on her bed and fitted my wrists and ankles with thick fleece and leather restraints. They were chained and locked fast to eyebolts on the floor. I truly could not move. I felt myself flirting with panic. Although there were only the two of us now in the room, I felt more embarrassed than ever and buried my head in the sheets. I didn't want to see what was coming.

Something coarse and thick swept over my back. It was a horse tail! Coral whisked it softly across my ass and then flicked it sharply on the same spot. It barely stung, but before I could let it register, another tender sweeping sensation floated over the same stinging spot. The tail felt completely different depending on how she stroked me.

"Look at what your next choices are," Coral said. Sitting in front of my nose were five whips: one knotted, one thick with many strips, one riding crop, one strap, and one paddle board like Sister Teresa used on our fifth grade class. I was a goody two shoes and never felt that paddle on my butt. Now I had a perverse desire to get it. "I want to try all of them," I said. "Just build up slowly to the meanest ones."

Coral built it up all right. She took each whip in turn, sliding it across my buttocks once just so I got the feel of its surface, then she hit me quickly, lightly—then she spiked it. She reached under me and pinched my clit between her fingers. That felt so good I pulled at my bonds as hard as I could. "You're teasing me!" I cried.

Of course she had to laugh. My ass was red now. The crop she used was a far cry from the horse feathers. It burned like a match. Below the waist, I felt like another body was taking over. When she reached for my cunt and pressed her knuckles inside me, I groaned and let her give me the hardest strokes. Her fucking me was the only thing that made it bearable.

I had to ask for a break. My tears were constant now, but my mind felt clear. "Coral, how am I supposed to take this pain? It's so intense. I don't know where to go with it."

She pushed my hair out of my face and helped me blow my nose. "Well, there are lots of ways to think about it. When I get hit, I like to think about deserving it, needing to be punished."

"I can't do that!" I choked. "I was just thinking the very opposite. . . all I can think of is that I don't deserve this. I didn't do anything wrong."

"Well, you can do it for Honey Lee. I know that's what she'd like."

"Yes, that's what O would do, but I'm too selfish for that."

"You can be selfish as well. A lot of people like to take the pain and connect the intensity to their clit or their nipples."

"Maybe. When you stroke my clit and fuck me, I appreciate the whip a little, because my cunt sucks the sensation right up."

My break was over. That cane, the five-foot bamboo cane, was still standing in the corner. I had a feeling I wouldn't be able to erotically connect any part of my body to *that*.

Coral traced her fingers over a little star of a welt on my left bottom cheek. It did indeed throb. She picked up her cane and drew its length through the crack of my ass. It was so hard and spiny. Then she cut it through the air like a thunderclap. When it snapped on my ass, my legs turned to jello and for the first time, I screamed. I screamed so loud I scared myself. It came down again and my heart flew out of my mouth.

"Coral, please, please, I can't do it, please, Jesus, I can't."

Maybe that's what I said, I don't know. All I remember is begging Coral to stop. She complied instantly.

She knew I'd reached my limit. She didn't carry out the rest of the punishment they'd threatened for all my earlier smarty-pants remarks. She unlatched my wrist cuffs in an instant and took me in her arms. There's nothing like being taken care of after you've been hurt like that. I wanted to cling to her for ages.

"Your lover is waiting for you," she said, untangling herself from my sweaty body and reaching down to unchain my legs. I wobbled out of bed and picked up my boots. Everything was so heavy.

"Coral, you're going to suffer terribly for what you did to me today." I knew that would make her happy.

I stood by the front window and gathered my things. Glancing down below, I saw that our car was still there, with Honey Lee inside. She was staring right up at our floor, with her mirrored sunglasses on. What had she been dreaming about, watching the window this whole time!

I don't think Honey has ever seen me so serene as when I got in the front seat. "You look like a saint," she said when I sat down.

"Yeah, well you know how religious experiences are," I whispered. I wasn't surprised when she pulled a long white scarf out of the glove compartment and told me to turn my head. She wrapped it around my eyes several times. I didn't even try to follow the car's direction. I felt nothing urgent, except the pulse of the stripes on my behind.

When we came to a stopping place, she led me down a narrow sidewalk and into a low-ceilinged room. We were back home. I could hear voices exclaim their admiration as I entered the room. Many hands, too many to count, reached out for my clothes and undressed me. They lifted me onto a soft bed, but I still couldn't tell how many or who they were. I was being kissed all over. Oil was being dribbled on my chest. I was massaged by countless fingers. Someone lifted my head and slipped in a cold piece of peach. I smelled the champagne just as the glass was pressed to my lips. A little of that spilled down my neck and then I felt a cool mouthful of the same liquid circle my nipple. I tried to count how many were there, and identify their voices, but it was impossible. They kept changing positions, and I couldn't concentrate on more than three sensations at a time. I was so wet and warm and stinging that I gave up trying to think at all.

But someone else started kissing me, deeply: Honey Lee. The other hands and tongues began to fade, and it wasn't just my imagination. The hundreds of fingertips were leaving me. Honey Lee never left my mouth, but the rest of my body became still.

She took off my blindfold. No one was left except for us.

"Are they going to come back? You tell me who they were!" I knew she wouldn't tell me. "How can I go out and work or call my friends when I have no idea who was here making love to me?"

Honey gave up nothing. "Did you like your birthday, Susie?"

The next week, I pulled a couple of handwritten envelopes out from among the bills piled in the mailbox. I opened the first one and found a polaroid of my friend Miranda doing something outrageous to my toes, surrounded by seven other busy pairs of hands. "Your feet were divine," she had written on the border. Similar envelopes followed.

"I wonder how many photographs like this are in circulation?" I said out loud. But O wouldn't have asked such a thing. She would have written her story in all its detail. And so I did.

SHINY PLASTIC DILDOS
HOLDING HANDS

My mummy told me
If I was goody
That she would buy me
A rubber dolly,
But Auntie told her
I kissed a soldier,
Now she won't buy me
A rubber dolly.

What would I do if I had a penis?

I would be very unhappy to have a penis on the body I possess now. It would ruin everything. Sometimes I think about a tail, wings, or claws, but a cock springing from beneath my soft belly would be a gross error. I would feel like a transsexual, caught in the wrong body.

What if I were a man? Then, of course, I'd have a penis. My friend Sarah Schulman wrote a story about a lesbian who wakes up one day with a penis. She ends up cruising in Central Park and meets a guy in the bushes who goes down on her. "Ann had always wanted to say 'suck my cock' because it was one thing a lot of people said to her, but she never said to anyone."

I'd like to say that, too. And if I were a man and *had* a cock, one of my favorite things would be waking up with an erection and feeling my lover's ass cup around me when she pushed back against my belly. Or maybe she'd straddle me, or wake me up by sucking me. Men always look blissful in the morning when awakened, and I'd like to feel that too. I used to have a girlfriend who turned rosy when I woke her up by sucking her nipples. Perhaps my envy comes entirely from the fact that I always wake up first. up first.

But consider the disembodied penis, the classic dildo I'm so fond of. I have lots and lots of dildos, and I have done everything I can think of with them, including strapping one on and whispering, "Suck my cock." Fucking, of course, is my main pleasure with dildos; I occasionally suck and, in the case of man-made materials, chew them. Other diversions include packing them in my jeans and melting them in saucepans to carve new shapes.

I realize I'm on the fringe with my dildo collection. Rubber dollies are still misunderstood. The world's most popular and durable erotic accessory, whether carved in ivory or organically grown and found in the Safeway cucumber bin, is more often than not derided as the palest of imitations.

I first became a dildo booster to alleviate the fears of some lesbian feminists that they would become magically heterosexualized by a toy phallus. I was speaking to a small audience about an intensely sectarian subject, I thought. But lesbian apprehension about plastic penises emerged as a mere by-product of the whole world's age-old disdain. The feminist anti-rubber critique is only modern window dressing.

The most common prejudice is that dildos are for old maids, lonely hearts, the hard-ups who lack a hard-on. Your typical dildo bigot was immortalized recently by my friend the cartoonist Spain, in a comic book called *Young Lust*. His straight male character/alter ego, suitably called THE SEXIST, ends his tirade against artificial penetration with this damning accusation: "So why do you want to put some dead plastic thing up in you when you can have something human and real up there, something that gets nice and hard for you?"

Why indeed? We had a big argument about it. Many a nice, live, human being enjoys the pleasures of fucking without a genuine dick, while those "lucky" couples with "real" things may find themselves performing passionless intercourse. A "real" dick may get hard, but it's not always nice.

After our go-round, I felt like writing the Dildo Fairness Doctrine. Separate fact from fiction. Raise world consciousness.

Fucking feels good—that's the basic premise of dildo popularity—and when it comes to penetration, why NOT have it your way? Using a dildo allows lovers to get it on in any shape, size, texture, or color. That's an eternity of fantasy material right there. Of course, dildos are the sweet revenge of every liberated size queen. Dildo selection is almost always about size, and careful comparison between carrots will undoubtedly teach ingenues the range of satisfaction from sassy and fat to long and slender.

My friend June, a gay immigrant to San Francisco, proudly displays her Adam II (seven by two inches) on the coffee table. She speaks like a woman who's weathered the accusations, and who still has held firmly to her plastic belief system.

"The idea that you should be orgasmically satisfied with your lover's precious fingers or tongue is romantic horse shit," she says. "No one would expect you to marry someone for the size of his cock or his fist! Yet we're expected to act as if love and a nice personality are all the equipment we need to have satisfying sex."

Voyeurism and vicarious pleasure are also no small part of dildo enjoyment. My thirty-eight-year-old neighbor Andrew is the proud owner of a dozen dildos. He found his first—a slightly bent butt plug—in a gym locker ten years ago. "At first I brought it home and made it a coffee table conversation piece. Then one day I was bored, so I changed its little battery and stuck it up my butt. I came so hard

I had to peel myself off the bed. It took me two weeks to get up the nerve to show it to my lover, but that's when I got my second lucky break. He already knew everything there was to know about dildos. . . . Nowadays it's more fashionable, or at least less unusual, to use dildos, because safe sex has this high profile—but that wasn't my original point of view."

What people *do* with dildos is different from the business of making and selling them, which is an industry all to itself. A typical "novelty" factory and warehouse is a block-long wholesaler's outlet in a Korean/black neighborhood of Los Angeles. The manufacturer, who has been in business for thirty years, prefers secrecy, in part because at this very moment, he's being prosecuted by a Texas grand jury for "interstate transportation of obscene goods." Texas is a state where ownership of more than six dildos is a crime; that makes you a dildo pusher. The commercial sex toy industry has always been under attack by Bible-thumping political opportunists. But if I were to criticize these businesses for anything, it wouldn't be for some ill-defined obscenity, or for any clear and present danger—it would be for their unwavering mediocrity and conservatism in making products for their market.

For decades, the handful of novelty manufacturers in the United States and in Hong Kong put out the same tired, pseudo-Caucasian rubber dicks, sometimes filled with air bubbles or covered with pock marks. They come in two basic sizes: huge and ridiculous. Women's sex toy shops—like Good Vibrations in San Francisco and Eve's Garden in New York—nagged commercial manufacturers for years before they came up with some alternative colors, textures, and sizes.

A West Indian inventor and holistic health practitioner in Brooklyn produced the first real innovation in dildo selection. His name is Gosnell Duncan, and he is the creator of Scorpio Products, a collection of silicone-mixture dildos in a fantastic array of shapes. They come in penis and fluted forms, and in lavender, creamy honey-colored, and deep brown shades.

Duncan pursued his invention because he was active in providing sexual information resources to disabled men who were impaired by erection dysfunction. He himself had a debilitating work accident as a young man. "I made these devices as an experiment. Then I heard from a couple of transsexuals in Canada who were interested in products made from the material I had created."

Duncan's new "devices" were expensive and hard to find. But they stood head and shoulders above anything else for sale, and they became tremendously popular. As an inventor and sex educator, Duncan was perhaps the first dildo manufacturer to take a sincere interest in his customers' desires and needs.

The gay leather shops in San Francisco and New York were another embryonic ground for sex toys. Leather-stitched dildos became popular. Sophisticated European latex designs, like the must-have Dutch inflatable dildo, were appealing to newcomers during the eighties dildo explosion.

I was caught in the dildo dilemma along with all the other lesbians shopping in women's sex stores. We found ourselves in the middle of a hurricane controversy over the "correctness" of re-appropriating the phallus. But the raised eyebrows just brought more curiosity-seekers out of the closet.

In the early eighties, my position at Good Vibrations afforded me the view of a sex-toy control tower: I kept track of arriving and departing attitudes. Sharon, one of my old customers, is a forty-something dyke who remembers her first time at the dildo counter in Good Vibrations. "It was 1985, and it seemed like I couldn't go into my five-woman house without landing in the middle of some argument over sex. It was a big mishmash of S/M and butch/femme, but right at the very bottom of it was this desire to fuck and be fucked. I bought my first dildo and harness in secret."

Sharon's memories stir more than mere nostalgia for dykes who are having their initial brush with lesbian cock-consciousness. Even the most non-judgmental woman is likely to burst into either laughter or moans when she first sees herself in a full-length mirror with a dildo strapped 'round her hips.

"I never thought of myself with a phallus," says my friend Lorraine, a gay junior high school teacher whose Sex Ed. classes have improved conceptually since she bought her first dildo. "I bought these toys quite naïvely, thinking it was fun, something unusual. But I wasn't at all prepared for how different I felt fucking my girlfriend with a dick instead of my hands. At first I felt ridiculous! Then, this wave of euphoria came over me, followed by an even bigger wave of shame. I've always thought of myself as androgynous, but in terms of a middle ground, not as a woman who had sharp masculine desires or any trace of masculine identity. I had to pinch myself the next morning to see if it was still me."

Gloria, who I met a few years later, is Lorraine's ex-lover. "I am your original lie-down femme," she boasts. "Lorraine got the cock to fuck me, and I loved it—it liberated her. It's so hard to drag butches out of the closet and sometimes a dildo is the only thing that gets the point across. I can take or leave fucking a man, but a woman with a cock has my full attention. It's not just the toy; a whole part of her personality comes out."

I had to ask if Gloria had ever flipped her butch lovers. "Well, a couple of times. I'm pretty romantic about who does what, and the only times I've felt really uninhibited using a strap-on was with inexperienced girls or straight women. I like the looks on their faces when they see my long hair, big tits, big erection. I would like to fuck a butch with my ten-inch, or even watch her fuck another butch, but I haven't met anyone broad-minded enough yet. . . ."

What Gloria and Lorraine have in common with heterosexual women is this: However irreverent her approach to a dildo, any woman is bound to confront what such a masculine symbol means to her body and desires. She may respond with humor and ten years down the road, she may have a hard time remembering what all the fuss was about. But she *will* deal with it. In a sense, her experience is analogous to what a straight man feels about dildos. He has to face his submissive, feminine, and sexually receptive qualities. He may wish for prostate stimulation without all the emotional baggage, but there's no way out of it.

Gay men, who traditionally appreciate any sort of phallic festivities, have the Dionysian advantage: They can enjoy dildos without the buy-one-and-get-an-identity-crisis dilemma. For a gay man, "something that gets nice and hard just for you" is of course the best treat. But if that same desirable man with a hard-on wants to have something up his butt while you suck him, who's going to throw him out of bed? True, this takes some imagination. And frankly, most gay men are in the same boat as everyone else when it comes to being fearful and suspicious of something out of the ordinary.

This may be the bottom-line resistance to dildos: They are *not* ordinary. And people who enjoy them do not think of themselves as "ordinary." Dildos are forever as provocative as they are inanimate. Some will be cherished like teddy bears; others are destined to be hacked into silly putty in a post-phallic temper tantrum.

It's like that popular bumper sticker about guns: "Dildos don't fuck people, people fuck people." A rubber dolly only has as many wonderful adventures as a mistress or master can conjure up.

POCKET DILDO GUIDE

Dildos you can find at any sleazy store:

The Ten-Inch Hunk: Orangey pink, huge, anatomically mythic. Always use a condom with this type; it's impossible to clean, because it's riddled with tiny holes and air bubbles. Cheap, but it does the trick.

The Double Dildo: Mushroom cock-heads at both ends of a long (fifteen- to eighteen-inch) rubber phallus. These are used pussy to pussy, or pussy to asshole, or ass to ass. One or both of you push/pull the dildo's middle to create the motion between you. It's harder to do than it looks. Very few couples have the compatible body types that jibe with this item, but if they do, they're hooked.

The Hollow Hunk: This hollow, hard plastic cock is designed to fit over a penis, giving a larger or lengthier look. The problem is you don't know how the device will feel around your penis until you try it. These things are inexpensive, so buy a few, and experiment at home.

The Hard Shiny Vibrating Dildo: Comes in a variety of sizes, from finger-long to pony ride. The battery-operated vibration is so weak that you are unlikely to feel more than a numb tingle. Let the batteries go dead and you can be perfectly happy with these smooth, easy-to-clean dildos, now available in decorator colors.

The Japanese Beaver: In the early eighties, Japanese sex toy manufacturers popularized a series of devices, especially for women, that consisted of a two-pronged pleasure attack: a clitoral vibrator that twigs out from a rotating dildo branch. Japanese law forbids the manufacturing of toys which resemble human genitalia, so these objects were designed to look like cute animals: beavers, bears, or kittens. Such cunning alternatives made a big splash in the American market, and now everyone makes them.

SPECIALTY DILDOS

Artistically produced, fluctuating in supply, and only in the best erotic boutiques:

The Silicone Dildo: This has a creamy texture, unlike the rubber device; it's easy to clean, and tempting to gnaw on. But watch your teeth, because the tiniest tear in a silicone product will spread quickly into a complete break, and there's nothing you can do to mend it. The producers of silicone dildos also have a thoughtful, hand-molded array of sizes, shapes, and colors. Scorpio Products, the granddaddy of silicone dildos, are available in a few erotic boutiques across the country. Dils for Does and Lickerish Ltd. are women-owned manufacturing companies; Dils for Does has silicone fantasies that range from a molded ballerina's leg to a baby's fist.

The Vagicizer or *The Vaginal Barbell*: Looks like a steel barbell for Barbie's playhouse. This item was marketed with all sorts of pompous claims about exercising women's vaginal muscles. Of course a woman can tone her pelvic muscles without devices of any kind (orgasms are the best exercise of all). But this pretty silver toy just plain feels great, for either vaginal or anal insertion. It's heavy and cool to the touch, high-tech in look.

The Lucite Dildo: Aesthetically more appealing than the usual "realistic" penis model, the Lucite dildo is made by large-scale manufacturers, but is not commonly stocked.

The Hawaiian Wooden Dildo: For the true collector or for someone who just appreciates a dildo as an *objet d'art*. A famous artist, whose works are displayed in the Louvre and MOMA, has a hobby: He collects gorgeous samples of native woods in tropical locations and carves them into undulating and phallic designs. He sells a limited number to Good Vibrations in San Francisco, where they retail at around a hundred dollars each. Beautiful and lasting love objects.

Black Latex from Europe: The certain *je ne sais quoi* that you've searched for everywhere might well be found in the inflatable black rubber dildo. This literally allows you to pump yourself to a climax. Or there's the spaghetti whip dildo, a sensual stick shift, topped with thin latex laces that feel more like a cool shower than a stinging whip. Very nice.

Rolling Pins, Summer Squash, and Tortoise Shell Hairbrushes: There's nothing as sentimental or dear as a dildo you picked from your own garden or fashioned from your very own medicine chest or kitchen cabinet. Get back to your roots.

RAPE SCENES

I remember the first time someone stuck his hand down my pants when I didn't want him to. My roommate and I were mugged and molested in San Francisco while walking home from a movie. What I remember most was that my assailant was a full head shorter than me. He looked to be about fourteen, and he had the tip of his knife pushed against my breastbone. I was scared stiff, unable to move, pleading. Our two mugger boys were so inexperienced themselves that one of them handed my roommate's key ring back to her so he could use both hands to unfasten her pants. She blew the silver whistle that hung off her keys, and as if she had fired a warning shot, the armed and dangerous brats scattered like rabbits. It was over. I felt like shit, and I continued to feel like shit for months. I moved out of that neighborhood.

I remember the first time I had a rape fantasy. I was quite young and had gotten my hands on a very naughty book. This naughty book was actually a serious volume on true tales of juvenile delinquency which I found in the library. One story described a teenage girl pinned to a cross, just like Jesus, on a grassy hill outside her suburb; all the boys in her school had their way with her. Another story was about a little girl who didn't obey her parents' warnings not to talk to strangers. She was kidnaped by a couple who sequestered her in their apartment and introduced her, day by day, to various sex acts which she first resisted and then (of course) became addicted to. I was attending Catholic school at the time and my head was already filled with stories of romantic martyrdom and the wages of sin. The juvenile delinquents' dramas played over and over again in my head at night as I rubbed myself through layers of sheets, pajamas and underwear, always coming very hard. I never left *that* neighborhood.

I did not acknowledge having masochistic or submissive turn-ons until I was in my twenties. In a feminist college course, our teacher asked us if we had experienced arousing rape fantasies. One girl tearfully raised her hand and said this was true for her. My heart started beating so fast it was all I could do to stay put. I was just as ashamed as she of these fantasies, but I would never have admitted them. Our professor was actually quite kind to her, if misinformed. She comforted the girl by saying that, as women, we had been brainwashed by the patriarchy to eroticize our subordination to men. She said these fantasies were very common, which is true, and that we could "overcome" them by exposing our fantasies to feminist analysis and by our increasing self-esteem.

She was dead wrong. In fact, I knew she was wrong later that same night. Despite my assertive self-confidence, rock-hard feminist analysis and weekly shift at the rape crisis hotline, I could still crawl into bed and successfully masturbate to those same disturbing fantasies that had aroused me since I was a child. Feminism and self-esteem had no more effect on my erotic hot spots than the communion wafers I used to take every Sunday, hoping they would wash away the devil's seed inside of me. Clearly, religion and linear politics were useless in explaining the unconscious and subversive quality of eroticism.

Two years later, I started reading about sexuality for the first time: the stuff that comes after the birds and the bees. At an airport newsstand, just before boarding, I picked up the mass market edition of Nancy Friday's *My Secret Garden* in idle curiosity. The back cover quoted some eminent psychiatrist who said the book revealed "the hidden content of our own sexuality." I wondered what it would reveal about me, other than that I was a hopeless pervert.

It was a long trip from L.A. to Detroit. In fact, I would say it was the most excruciating five hours I have ever spent in the air. My face was scarlet; my floatable seat cushion was wringing wet. Friday quoted her "first name only" correspondents—Marie, Debbie, Jessica—describing fantasy after fantasy on subjects I had never spoken out loud: incest, anal sex, erotic kidnapings, dog lickings, gang bangs, screwing on altars and panting in total darkness with nothing on but a blindfold. As flabbergasted as I was that these women came from every background and corner of the map, I recognized that I had been arousing myself with similar themes for as long as I could remember. I never consciously said to myself, "Oh, I think I'll fantasize about my sex slave circus tonight." But each time I climaxed, at the moment of truth, those tigers and cowering slave girls flashed through my mind. The whip cracked.

I was one of Nancy's kids. According to the book's cover copy, I was one of a million women who read this book and, I assume, had a similar reaction. Either we were a million perverts clutching our grimy handbooks in shame, or these sexual fantasies were as normal as apple pie.

I had never really thought about what created an erotic fantasy. I thought a sex fantasy was some *Tiger Beat* scenario where you scored a dream date with this month's current tanned celebrity. I had masturbated since I was eight, but when I squeezed my eyes shut and bore down so hard on my arm that my fingers went numb, I never saw Paul Newman drift across my orgasmic screen. Or Mick Jagger. Or Bianca Jagger, for that matter.

Nancy Friday broke down the closet door of female sex fantasy by presenting the unfiltered erotic confessions of hundreds of women. Unfortunately, she also insisted on providing, in the same pages, her misguided analysis of female sexuality. Her lengthy introductions to each section of fantasies were designed to legitimize the book's intent, but sad to say, her stab at explaining why women are aroused by this taboo material was an intellectual disaster area. On the one hand, she was a feminist who believed her respondents were thriving, healthy women who had a lot of guts to speak out like this. On the other hand, she hinted that the whole lot of them had seriously ruptured relationships with their mothers. Or fathers. Or maybe society at large. It was pop psychology at its most awful.

Instead of providing the delicate framework needed to understand how erotic fantasies come from all manner of triggers, both deeply personal AND cultural, Friday tried to read fantasies like they were Tarot decks. Oh, you have a lesbian fantasy? That must be the "longing to be close to mother" card. Every time I read one of her explanations, I felt like someone was trying to stuff my foot into a shoe that didn't have a prayer of fitting. Later, when I recommended the book to friends, I issued strict instructions: Read the fantasies ONLY and draw your own conclusions.

Friday has continued to collect fantasies since *My Secret Garden* and its sequel, *Forbidden Flowers*, came out in the mid-seventies. She finally has compiled an anthology of fantasies for the nineties: *Women on Top*. As you can guess from her title, she not only has new stories to share, but she also claims that women's lives and wet dreams have changed extraordinarily since she did her first interviews twenty years ago.

On one score she's right. Most of the women in her new book are young—the end of the baby boomers. Their attitude toward masturbation is utterly matter-of-fact. One of the rare fifty-year-old contributors ends her fantasy with the exclamation of a post-feminist convert: "Masturbation is GREAT." The younger women consider sexual satisfaction a completely reasonable expectation in their lives.

Nancy is full of evidence to document the End of the Good Girl Era. Sex toys are commonplace in her respondents' bedrooms, and in their fantasies, these sometimes take on Terminator-style proportions, as in one story about a woman who imagines herself being penetrated and stroked along a relentless conveyer belt.

The fantasies are just as wild when they come from virgins as when they're from women with plenty of experience. "Connie," who has never had sex with anyone besides the boyfriend she met in fifth grade, tells a hot story about her turn-on for cops in uniform. She imagines being pulled over in her car and given a thorough pat-down. "[He] titillates my clit like a marble in oil."

Friday's research is an erotic marathon. The Gorilla Science Lab Experiment alone, where the woman scientist seduces her subject, is enough to send you to bed for a week. It becomes clear, reading story after story, that no territory is so fantastic that it cannot arouse you or remind you of your own provocative daydreams. Each woman prefaces her fantasy with a little information about her real life, making it obvious how normal, how common it is to fantasize about the bizarre, the taboo, the things that in real-life circumstances would trouble us, frighten us, or maybe just make us laugh. Erotic fantasies take the unbearable and unbelievable issues in life and turn them into orgasmic gunpowder.

Switching genders was a new issue in *Women on Top*, although I know women who were fantasizing this sort of thing long before Friday published it. One woman explains that when she massages her clitoris she imagines it growing "larger and larger until it is the size of a penis. I imagine I can feel the sensation of a man during intercourse. I also imagine that the man is having sex with me. . . hence I can feel the sensation of both partners at the same time."

As excited as Friday is to show off new fantasies where women experiment with men's traditional roles, her political agenda is still at odds with her story material. What she wants to prove is that today's groovy heads of households have dumped those nasty old oppressive rape fantasies in favor of turning the tables on their oppressors—dominating men and loving it. "Women in *My Secret Garden* who may have had very controlling natures in reality invented elaborate fantasies of rape," Friday recalls. "It was all they dared themselves. Then once *My Secret Garden* was published, overnight the rape fantasy was rejected by the women in this book who wanted total power over and domination over men."

Oh, horse feathers. Women are not newcomers to fantasies where they wield the sexual power, nor have we abandoned fantasies of being ravished just because this is the macha nineties. A woman's place in her job or home is no forecaster of what her fantasies may be. How can Friday not know this yet? A woman or man CEO can have the most hair-raising rape fantasy on the block, and it will have nothing to do with lack of courage. A willing submission is every bit as powerful as a domination fantasy. And in our fantasies, no matter how much we struggle to deny it, we control every frame. Whether we are standing tall in thigh-high boots or are breathless on our knees is simply a matter of our well-lubricated position. As Friday knows from her survey of men's fantasies in *Men In Love*, men have submissive fantasies in even greater numbers than women. So spare us the pseudo-feminist bible stories.

Friday devotes a full chapter to "Women Controlling Men," and while it is certainly a delightful treasure trove (Lou Ellen and her fifteen well-endowed male housekeepers are particularly fabulous), it is downright irritating that Friday buries the numerous submissive and masochistic fantasies in chapters whose titles don't hint at their contents.

Lesbian fantasies get the worst treatment. Friday insists that "all fantasies with other women begin and end with tenderness." Then, in the very next fantasy, a girl named Brett says her favorite fantasy is to be dominated by a group of ruthless bulldykes. Not one particle of tenderness is mentioned. In many of the other lesbian fantasies, the feminine attraction is bitchy or masculine rather than narcissistic or maternal.

Friday's prejudiced image of lesbianism as the last word in sisterly, dewy-eyed breast worship is dead wrong. She misses the variety of gay life, and the fantasies she has collected don't accurately represent the spectrum of lesbian desire.

Friday took all the fantasies which didn't fit her new "dominant woman theory" and scattered them throughout the book in the most unlikely places. I had to search and search to find the very best innocent babysitter fantasy ("I am babysitting two boys. They decide to play Indians and tie me up. Here their father comes in. . . .") which was stuck in a chapter called "Women with Bigger Appetites than Their Men." If this was *my* anthology, I would have had chapter titles like "Sweet Innocent Babysitters," "Secret Spy Agents," and "True Tales from the Catholic Church."

In her claim that women are now "on top" in their sexual fantasies, Friday cultivates a dangerous party line. She imagines that women's economic independence is somehow tied to the content of our sexual fantasies. We don't need to make a case for feminism by claiming that women are now entertaining new improved ringmaster or revenge fantasies. This kind of thinking unwittingly censors the diversity and complexity of real women's fantasies. It is the same as my women studies teacher claiming that only unliberated women have rape fantasies, and that as soon they get their consciousnesses raised, those ugly stains will wash right out.

What really happens when you get your consciousness raised is that you can't be afraid of your fantasies any longer. You see the difference between your real life anxieties and limitations vs. your potential to go to any extreme in fantasy. Now *that* is empowering. Erotic dreams certainly communicate powerful and very personal messages. But to read them as if they were tea leaves amounts to some pretty tacky fortune telling.

We can't assume that certain labels lead to certain behavior and vice versa. After I was mugged and fingered by the fourteen-year-old prick, I had several fantasies. In one, my revenge fantasy, I walked in on him at home during Sunday dinner and shamed him in front of his family. His mother told him to get out, that he could never come back again. In another fantasy, I imagined my "if only" scenario, where I raised my long arm, disregarding his blade cutting into my chest, and decked him. I spit on him lying in the street, and the blood from where he nicked me dripped into his eyes.

But in the third fantasy, he kept fucking me with his hands, and I was frozen, naked on the sidewalk. He talked to me nasty, he was arrogant, and he teased the knife against my nipples. Neighborhood people gathered; he invited them to take his place.

I had this last fantasy twice, both times culminating in orgasm. Then it became impossible to conjure up. My old rape fantasies from childhood came back in its place.

A year later, I moved back into the old neighborhood, the "scene of the crime," but I was smarter and, in a first for me, I was territorial. Welcome to *my* neighborhood— all of it.

STRIP TEA

You know how hard it is to get good service nowadays. Chivalry is a corpse, discretion is unheard of, and elegance—elegance is currently defined by advertisements for Bob's Discount Furniture. A well-bred woman might spend her entire maturity never once hearing the words "May I be of service to *you*?"—although she may spend her life waiting on others, particularly children and men. Such a predicament could make strong women weep and gnash their teeth, but when the going gets tough, the tough throw a party. A very unusual party.

One month ago, I received an invitation to attend a salon of women artists. We were offered an occasion to read aloud, sketch, and indulge ourselves in a very proper high tea. Most intriguing of all, the invitation promised we would be served our scones and punch by naked slaveboys who would not speak unless spoken to. The aspect of social nudity was of course titillating, but would ordinary men actually keep their lips buttoned for an approximately five-hour affair? That had to be seen to be believed. I wouldn't have missed it for the world.

Upon arrival, I was indeed greeted by a nude doorman who took my coat. Alas, he was the only servant in sight, and in the meantime, guests were arriving by the score. What a delightful group of invitees they were, too. If I had been able to get a simple cup of hot Earl Grey, my afternoon would have been complete. But unfortunately, although the company was sublime and the concept impeccable, only two slaveboys were on hand to provide services, and despite their best intentions, I don't think either of them had ever so much as poured a cup of decaf.

The guests were also tragically uneducated in the fine art of being served in splendor. Though a couple of us were dressed in literary salon frocks, some came in sweatpants. One lovely woman offered to get up and fetch me a scone, and when I gently reminded her she was a guest at this soirée, she pleaded with me, "It doesn't matter, I'm a bottom in real life." Ah yes, but real life is what we are trying to escape.

The ultimate affront was the vision, midway through the party, of an attractive girl on her knees actually giving the so-called slaveboy a neck massage! It was all I could do to restrain myself from slapping both of them to their senses.

I departed with my friend, Laura Miller. We reviewed the afternoon and agreed it had been a wonderful, yet insufficient, experience. Wouldn't it be perfect to have a party like that in a grand mansion, with slaveboys who looked like Greek gods and served like altar boys?

"I'll dream of it," I told her as we parted, but Laura wasted no time in wistfulness.

The very next day, she called me. "My friend Amy Wallace, the novelist, has a beautiful home in the Berkeley hills, and she would love to hostess the kind of tea party we have in mind. The living room is absolutely Byronic, and there are even special servants' quarters."

I blinked. The first hurdle, getting out of our filthy, tiny, crime-ridden neighborhood apartments, had been overcome in the twinkling of a phone call. Now where on earth would we find the slaveboys?

Laura is the book review editor at the *San Francisco Weekly*, where personal ads of all persuasions abound. She agreed to place an ad for four weeks, but I had my doubts about getting much of a response to anything so bizarre. I was more confident that in my Rolodex I would find lots of liberated boys who would love to serve us tea.

Little did I know the raw nerves our search would

scratch. I got my first glimpse of the normal red-blooded American male reaction during a trip to my mechanic. "Look what I'm up to," I said, pulling into the garage and waving my carefully typed personal ad:

> Genteel and Bohemian gathering of women writers requires comely slaveboys to serve at our tea party. You will serve nude and will not speak unless spoken to. Standards are high. Food and beverage experience a must. No sex. Please send photo and qualifications to Madam Tea Party.

"What the fuck do I want with waiting on a bunch of broads?" asked Jake, leaning against his greasy desk. "You're not paying anything for this? No way."

Some little lost feminist emotion in me snapped. "Women have been waiting on you from the time you were born," I said. "And you can't imagine switching sides for a couple of hours?"

The next week, I saw Jake again, and he asked how my search was going. The ad had not yet appeared, and I was getting nowhere.

My gay friends said they wouldn't have any fun waiting on women. "Why not?" I asked. "Whatever happened to your sense of classic theater? This isn't a pick-up scene, it's the tea to end all teas!"

My straight friends, even the most sympathetic, went into a panic about penis size and fantasized far more permanent humiliation than anything I had in mind. "I wouldn't have called you if I didn't think you were gorgeous," I told one friend. "If you think this is going to ruin your career, how do you imagine the richest men in America get away with all their shenanigans at the Bohemian Grove?"

But all my reassuring retorts were in vain. Jake felt a little sorry for me, and maybe, just maybe, he was intrigued. He took me for a spin on his Harley and, halfway down the freeway, yelled the most encouraging words I'd heard yet: "I don't have a tan."

The Sunset neighborhood fog closed in around us. "It doesn't matter," I yelled back. "No one has a tan anymore."

But fate was about to turn her touch-tone head. The Wednesday paper hit the streets. I was so pessimistic I didn't plan to check the answering service or the mailbox for a couple of days. But Laura called me only hours after the *Weekly* was on the stands. "Get your pen ready; you've got to call these two. The first one's a European model and the other one works at the Fairmont Hotel."

"We got two calls?" I was stunned.

"We got six calls," she answered, "but the others sounded like geeks." She rattled off the promising phone numbers.

We got over one hundred calls and letters in two weeks. I believe that is what is called a staggering response. The photos and descriptions offered a textbook case in broken stereotypes. Car dealers from San Mateo, computer millionaires from Marin, professional leather slaves who could only be contacted through their mistresses, and surfer dudes who could only be contacted though their bartenders. Punk boys, bus boys, sailor boys, and above all, would-be, wanna-be, I'll-do-anything-to-be your ever lovin' slaveboys. Wow. Now we had to interview them.

My partner in the highly sensitive interview process was our fourth hostess, Lisa Palac. Lisa was brave enough to offer her living room for our on-site questioning, and she made no bones about the necessity of nude auditions. "But how do we even bring it up without sounding like sleazebags?" I asked. I could not see past the embarrassment.

But I did know who to ask, someone who specialized in frequent nude auditions, and with that in mind I headed over to the Mitchell Bros. O'Farrell Theater, one of the last great strip clubs. I went to see Vince, who manages the dancers' schedules. He was completely laid back. "It's simply professional, like a casting call," he said. "You ask them all your questions first, then you tell them you'd like to take a Polaroid of them undressed, and that's it. Tell them to put their clothes back on after you take the shot."

I hadn't even considered that it might be harder to make them get dressed than undressed. If our attitude was the key to smooth interviewing, I decided we should prepare a few questions on a form and devised the soon-to-be-notorious Slaveboy Questionnaire.

"Do you have experience serving tea?

Hors d'oeuvres?

How about hand or foot massage?

Brushing hair?

Painting nails?

Building and tending fires?"

The applicants were informed that the costume would be a simple bow tie, black shoes and matching socks.

Of course, we were interested in why a man would want to serve at our party.

The most common motive expressed by the men was the excitement of being chosen to please a special group of women. For some, the idea that we were all writers was especially glamorous. One restauranteur recalled that he had seen a zillion parties where naked girls danced for Shriners, but never the other way around—it bothered him a little. However, guilt was not typical of our interviewees.

One particularly frank applicant, a sixty-year-old merchant seaman, said, "I have been a male chauvinist all my life. In recent years I have come to acknowledge that women are humanoidal types as well, with the same needs and desires as anyone else. . . ." However, in his same letter, he stated, "There is no greater turn-on to me than a buxom, dominant woman."

Of course, we had to remind all our potential slaveboys that our guests were not necessarily dominant, or buxom,

49

or in need of anything besides a piping hot cup of tea, served with quiet elegance. For this, we had a disclaimer: "This is not a play party, nor a professional group. We are not interested in disciplining, humiliating, or topping you at the party. If you find yourself uncomfortable at the party, you may speak to one of the hostesses and make a quiet departure. If the hostesses believe you are behaving inappropriately, you will be asked to leave."

The boys were then graded on Face, Body, Grace, Service Experience and that ever-important swing vote, Personality. I never realized before this process that I have the unfettered ability to judge people solely on their looks. It is a form of discrimination I have avoided my whole life, and yet here was a case where, in selecting a man who would not say anything more than "Cream or sugar?", I had to pay as much attention to his pecs as I did to his poise.

Men, unlike women in this situation, are not the least bit abashed to apply for the job whether or not they are physically attractive. One man wrote that the most that could be said for his appearance was that small children did not run from him screaming. Unfortunately for him, his honest and amusing qualities were not enough to overshadow our search for the perfect Adonis.

Two men got erections during the interview, and with our standard tea mistress composure, we paid no particular attention to them. Three slaveboys came in French maid outfits, which were quite precious, but we were very strict about our *Boys only* policy. One brought roses (extra points), one whined that he didn't see why he had to provide his own bow tie (immediate reject), and one had a résumé with the most impeccable statement of purpose: "An emphasis on service that puts your needs, not mine, uppermost in my mind." Music to our ears.

In the end, we picked the following six:

K. was a Bon Jovi look-alike, the only one who had been "around the scene," as he put it, familiar with the nuances of submissive etiquette. P. was our dining room dream come true, an Italian American who serves at one of the most luxurious restaurants in town. T. was indisputably the most charming man we met, with a proper British accent that made us want to give him special dispensation to say a few words. J., my only personal friend to respond to the call for comely menservants, had excellent massage skills, sure to compensate for what he lacked in scone service. R. was Hawaiian/Chinese, one of our youngest servers, and won our hearts in his interview when he turned his chin up and closed his eyes for his interview photo. "Just like a choirboy," I exclaimed. "I *was* a choirboy," he said. Instant winner. Finally, S., our blond, tan L.A. kid, who won his place only because he wrote a follow-up letter saying he would be the best slaveboy ever, summed up his interest with the Gestalt that he thought it would be a "real trip."

Now that our slaveboy acquisition was complete, I faced an unexpected problem: our two dozen guests were not exactly RSVPing *en masse*. Now mind you, I only asked women writers of the finest bearing and Bohemian, open-minded standards. But when I called a close friend whom I expected would be picking out her hat and gloves as we spoke, she surprised me with the awful truth. "I don't know about this kind of treatment," she said. "I would never approve of naked women waiting on men, so why should I care to endorse the reverse?"

"Believe me," I told her, "these fellows applied only out of the most fervent self-interest. . . . I'm not asking you to kick them; I'm asking you to enjoy a cup of tea without having to lift a finger!"

If there ever were a case to prove how ridiculous the idea of reverse sexism is, this kinky tea party was it. Women are utterly unaccustomed to having their needs anticipated, and their desires understood and attended to without speaking a word. Amy told me afterwards that even though she grew up in a very wealthy and doting family, she had never before experienced being waited on hand and foot.

Now, many men will protest that they have never had this experience either, but only because they take service for granted. Who cleans their houses? Cooks their favorite meals? Imagines what they'll feel like when they come home? How they would like to be touched? Very likely someone feminine, as that is what femininity is bred for— nurturing and forethought. For the sexes to turn the tables on this state of affairs doesn't result in an equal reversal. In their new positions, men and women do not imitate their original role models, but rather wonder and wander in the extravagance of changing hats.

Others of my peers were more blunt and less politically correct about their fears. "What if one of them hands me a cucumber sandwich and I'm eye level with his ding-dong?"

"The attention is not on them," I insisted. "The attention is on the women, who—if they follow the dress code to the letter (dresses or tuxes only)—should be far more stimulating to your eyes."

Another vexing query came from a couple of my lesbian friends, who failed to see how being waited on by nude men would be anything less than nauseating.

"This is not a party about erotic preference!" I repeated. "If it were, *I* would be the naked slavegirl and all the women would be in cowboy boots. This is a radical social event," I continued. "These men will certainly not be eye-sores and, as for cruising, you won't find a more intoxicating gathering than the guest list we have drawn up."

Indeed, the sixteen women who did attend were all beauties, intellectually and visually. Rupa arrived as Cleopatra, with a golden snake headdress and sandals. Lily wore a corset laced over the most mind-shattering body ever sprung from the foam. Honey Lee wore a tuxedo like she was born to it, and Susan's creamy curves spilled out of a purple patent leather strapless. I myself started out in a black leather skirt that laced up the back, but ended up in nothing but my slip and my straw hat with the yard of veil. I got awfully hot.

My friend Tom O'Conner made the most exquisite feast for us: lox and strawberries and madeleines and nouvelle sandwiches and three different kinds of scones. Photographer Michael Rosen turned Amy's upstairs library into a Victorian portrait studio. Any exhibitionist could take a slaveboy in tow and sit for a formal photograph, her hands clasped primly and her feet kissed with appropriate photogenic fervor. I asked that Michael be nude too, but I drew the line at the cook—the position of ultimate dominance.

I believe our finest hours were the literary review, where several of our poets stood before the fire and burned suitable prose into our ears. Much of it was so erotic that I could barely concentrate on the lovely slave loosening my stockings from my garter. He rolled them down to warm my bare feet with oil, and my toes grazed the soft hair on his chest as he rolled and squeezed them. Very distracting. My hair was brushed until it shone by our blond S., who unaccountably disappeared two-thirds of the way through the party. In a shocking kitchen gossip revelation, J. later told me that S., "didn't think the babes were hot enough." All I can say is that he combed my every strand with utmost sincerity.

At one point R. came up to me in distress; beneath the kitchen window, he'd spied a group of men scrutinizing the house. "Oh them, they're just architecture students," Tom said. But the postman was another story. He took one look, then another, then ran as fast as he could.

I don't think I really relaxed until the end. No matter how many massages or sips of brandy-laced tea, I didn't feel I could take my skirt off until the final hour, when we toasted all the company, particularly the servants, and went upstairs for a final hostess/slaveboy photo.

"Do you think you could all lift me up, like a human cradle?" I asked my five remaining angels. And to P., at my right, "Could I claw at your chest just for the camera?"

I collapsed as beautifully as possible into their ten strong arms. What a day. The youngest *and* the oldest guests left with the words that they had never been to such an elegantly wonderful party in their lives. How silly were those who rejected our invitation in fear of sexual pressure or humiliation! Has everyone but we sixteen souls forgotten the meaning of style? The meaning of fabulous? How was the Bay Area supposed to keep an avant-garde reputation if a few enlightened perverts didn't work their fingers to the bone?

I called my dear friends, Laura, Lisa and Amy, the next day. "I have only one regret," I said. "Right there at the end, when all of the boys held me up to the camera? I changed my mind about our rules. I would have loved a bit of sex right then."

A GOOD BUTCH IS HARD TO FIND:

Masculinity in the Nineties

When I speak in public about my appreciation of pornography, I look very much like a woman—long hair, lipstick, and a pretty dress. But the words coming out of my mouth express a frankness and confidence about sex traditionally associated with masculinity. Sometimes men tell me, "You get away with murder because you're a woman. If *I* stood up and said the same things you say about sex, I'd be crucified."

I tell them I wish they would get up the nerve to talk about what turns them on. I don't think they'd be booed. I would find it refreshing. When are men going to stop being so easily shamed about their sexuality?

Masculinity in the nineties has been erotically revived and challenged from unexpected quarters: women and gays. A lot of heterosexual men find this ridiculous, offensive, and even amazing. After all, what does being a man have to do with girls and queers?

A man is many things, not the least of which is his sexual style. The classic image of masculine sexiness requires handsome beauty, strength, a clear steady gaze, and a bit of the devil. Anyone, regardless of sexual preference, can both appreciate and attain these qualities. While many heterosexual men take for granted the erotic presentation of masculinity, gay men have built a whole aesthetic upon it—first in gay pornography, then in mainstream popular culture. Who's to say what came first—the *Honcho* centerfold or the Marlboro man?

And women? Female masculinity, always present but up to now suppressed, is the nineties taboo of choice. A woman's allure is only made more striking when she counterpoises masculine costume or gestures against her feminine body. When Madonna grabs her crotch and pulls, gay, straight and bi hearts beat a little faster. Women have discovered that masculine boldness gets attention. Bulldaggers still aren't beauty queens, but the femmes who adore them have picked up a few tips about the beauty of female masculinity. The rest of the world could do the same.

All this cosmetic turmoil and serious re-evaluation of sex appeal didn't originate in a fashion magazine. The past few decades have seen outrageous challenges to male and female roles. The so-called new age consciousness emphasized the possibilities of what men could be "if they tried." If Joe Chauvinist felt guilt about sexism, he now had the opportunity to apologize for his "penis privileges."

But somehow the apologies and puppy dog-shame were no more appealing than white liberal guilt about racism. What irked feminist women the most about new age "feminist" men were the numbers of them who were all talk and no risk, no guts, and not so incidentally, no sex. Go hate your penis someplace else.

It seems that many men—liberal, new age, and neo-conservative—have responded to an old-fashioned puritanical drive to succeed materially, no matter what the cost. In the case of my generation, the cost was sex. Your average WASP-man ignored his erotic feelings and abandoned his masculine presentation altogether.

Men slamming the closet door on their sexuality has not challenged the institution of sexism one iota. No woman is going to get a better job, or walk home safely at night, just because Joe Blow burned all his girly magazines and told his lover and friends that sex isn't the most important thing. *Getting laid* is not the most important thing, but sexuality—one's desires and erotic identity—is precious and priceless. When heterosexual women discover the pricelessness of sexuality, they often become mystified and frustrated, because men do not seem equally interested in enlarging their own sexual sophistication.

To be blunt, women hungry for sexy masculinity find men either unattractive workaholics or pathetic apologists for the male condition. The exceptions to the rule are problematic as well. We have the die-hard male chauvinist pigs who can always be counted on to be Don Juans in the bedroom and gentlemen in the drawing room—but rarely with the same women. Their vicious double standard seems joined at the hip to their masculine charm and imagination. If we attack their ugly arrogance, they pack up their hard-ons and go home to mommy.

The other exception is found in a straight women's joke circulating for at least twenty years: "If I like him, he's either married—or gay." While gays have been dismissed by straight men as effeminate poofs, women have noticed that something else is afoot. The most mainstream erotic images of masculinity in the nineties *all* originate from the gay aesthetic, found in both slick fashion magazines and gay pornography.

All the trends in contemporary male fashion, body building and body enhancement have blossomed from gay male subculture as well. The Calvin Klein advertisements are elegant parodies of a hard-core spread in *Blueboy,* a gay men's beefcake rag. The whole presentation of the rugged and gorgeous, strong-but-silent type—Clark Gable *and* the Mapplethorpe nude—is an idealized gay fantasy. It's Over the Top Butchness; it's hardly real, but then femmes and queens alike have known for a long time how much work it takes to be "real" in the beauty game.

Ask the men who make sex appeal their profession. They know the devotion of the gay world to the ideal of beauty. When Arnold Schwarzenegger tells the story of his climb from Mr. Universe to Mr. Movie Star, he keeps quiet about one interesting fact: Body building and Hollywood are nurtured, worshipped and populated by a homosexual grassroots. He wouldn't be where he is today if he didn't show respect for the gay source of his aesthetic.

Men schooled in the gay aesthetic are irrepressibly romantic about what is classically beautiful in the male figure and masculine values. Mature (but untutored) straight men also have romantic models—Arnold Schwarzenegger, Kevin Costner and James Bond—but these matinee idols are meant to be watched, not emulated. Young straight men are often likely to dress and act like their heroes; but as the inertia of anti-sexual responsibilities slows them in later years, their enthusiasm for a male sexual aesthetic takes a beating. Part of a gay man's maturity is developing his own interpretation of the masculine erotic. But for the traditional heterosexual young man, masculine romance and beauty are childish things, to be put away in the task of becoming a husband, a father, a responsibility-taker. The nuclear family ideal does not include sexual vitality and maturity.

In the seventies, we took a blowtorch to the rigidity of nuclear family conventions. We talked about yin and yang and the future of androgyny. But androgyny unfortunately became known as sameness, blandness, an absence of distinction. We need a new word to make our specific feelings clear. "Genderfuck"—our retort to genderlessness—is the word that best expresses the nineties renewal of the seventies queries about androgyny. No one wants you in your Mao Zedong pants suit any more. "Faux equality" has been exposed as compromise and conformity. It's the difference between the girl-thing and the boy-thing that makes androgyny so fascinating to begin with.

The beauty and strength of masculine eroticism is arousing in whomever embraces it, whether it's a handsome dyke or the latest macho screen idol. Perhaps the sexiest thing is the courage to embrace your style and the commitment to show yourself as sexual—no apologies. When we pit our prescribed roles against our erotic desires, the desires tend to lose out—we are, after all, the country that knows how to "just say no," particularly to sex. Sexuality is always the last priority, in education, in entertainment, and most personally, in our relationships. It's as if eroticism was only important for teenagers or during the first few weeks of an affair.

Women's and gay liberation led girls and queers to demand more sexual satisfaction and expression in our lives. We got it, too. Now it's time for so-called "straight guys" to liberate their sexual fantasies—or risk perpetually being left behind. The nineties will be sexually demanding on men—not to "perform," but to identify and express their erotic masculine and feminine qualities. Go ahead—call it Butch Pride.

THE VIRTUAL ORGASM

I didn't think we were going to have an out-of-body experience over dinner. In fact, I was surprised that Perry could answer the phone with so much pasta bulging in her cheeks.

"Hi there, this is Lacy," she breathed through her nose into the receiver. She automatically flashed five fingers across the table to her partner.

"What does that mean?" I whispered to Callie. I'd never seen a phone sex call in progress before.

Callie didn't bother to keep her voice down. "Five minutes. Watch the clock and we'll see if she gets him off in five minutes."

Perry had her whole mouth free now and was purring into the handset. "I'm a 38C-25-36," she said, tapping her Birkenstocks against my chair. Perry's hips haven't seen thirty-six inches in about ten years, and if she told one more whopper like that, I might blow my marinara sauce out my nose. . . .

"That's right," Perry said again, "a C cup, and—oh my!" she let the receiver dangle. "That wasn't even a minute."

"But he still pays for fifteen minutes minimum," Callie said, reciting the rules of their homegrown operation. She was more interested in impressing me with the financial facts than with the mechanics of sexual fantasy.

"That man didn't talk to *you*," I said, looking harder at Perry's princess phone than I did at her. I wasn't criticizing, I was simply in awe. "He talked to an hourglass figure with a breathy little voice who made him climax so hard he didn't even have a chance to say good-bye."

60

"Oh, it's me all right. It's me every time." Perry pulled a noodle taut between her fingers. "Welcome to futuresex, Miss Sexpert. You can be any BODY you want to be on a fiber optic network. But there's always a piece of me in every blonde, redhead and stunning brunette I deliver over the phone lines."

Perry and Callie introduced me to their phone sex service six years ago, when such an erotic outlet was fairly new. Fiber optics have come a long way since then. In the not-so-distant future, Perry will be able to "show" her customers as well as tell them all about her brassiere collection. Not only will she give them a picture, she will show them in 3-D: a technology that has been dubbed virtual reality—"virtual" because it seems to be absolutely real—but *isn't*.

Using virtual reality systems, we will literally be able to dial alternate realities, placing ourselves in meeting places and adventures of our own design. VR is not pie in the sky, either; it's happening right now, predominantly on the frontier of California's Silicon Valley.

"Virtual reality is simply a living environment created inside a computer," explains my friend Richard Kadrey, a sci-fi novelist. "You wear headgear and what's called a data glove. The headgear contains video projectors—basically two TV sets—that shine in your eyes and wrap around so that you have 3-D vision. Your hand in the glove can manipulate objects in the simulated environment, which can be anywhere and everything."

"This makes flying coach completely obsolete!" I cried. I started calculating how many years it would be before these VR systems were priced down for the common woman's budget.

Richard shook his head at me. "People are getting jazzed about this the way they did about computers in the fifties. It sounded like the Jetson Family. We'd all have helicopters; no one would be driving cars anymore. People talk a lot about VR, but in fact it barely exists. It's a very primitive technology.

"Let's say we're in this room," he continued, "and there are some teacups on this table."

"Virtual teacups, right?" I asked. "That I can see with my headgear?" He nodded, impatient to explain the best part.

"So my gloved hand, the disembodied hand, reaches down to pick up a cup. There are actually little studs in the glove so that when my hand wraps around the cup, I can feel something *like* a cup. But that's as far as we've gotten."

"So if it were a cup of hot tea, I couldn't feel the warmth?"

"No, you wouldn't."

"I'd just feel the shape of a cup."

"Right. And you couldn't tell the difference between that cup and this soft sofa. You couldn't tell that the sofa has a different surface tension. You wouldn't be able to tell that this is cotton and that's ceramic."

Richard's blow-by-blow description was a little disappointing but still intriguing. Virtual reality was either going to be the most mind-expanding communication device ever dreamed of, or as predictable and over-rated as the latest ride at the amusement park. What exactly was VR being used for right this minute, besides coffee table demonstrations?

R.U. Sirius is the very serious editor of *Mondo 2000*, a magazine devoted to imagination and computer technology, in particular to the realm of "cyberspace," the term coined by novelist William Gibson to describe the space you enter in virtual reality. R.U. explained to me that VR has been used in its most sophisticated form by the Defense Department and NASA.

"The Defense Department has the most advanced tele-robotic, long distance computer scanning equipment," he said. "That's what they used in Iraq. It was a 'virtual' war, which may be the dead opposite of the technoeroticism you're interested in."

"What is a 'virtual' war?"

"They've modeled the territory, so you can actually get human beings out of the loop. It takes very little human intelligence to fly a smart bomb mission. They strap on goggles, see where they're going and where they're going to drop bombs. It's a mapping system."

But the war experts are not the only ones calculating the possibilities for virtual technology. Sirius rattled off a list of contenders in the burgeoning virtual marketplace like he was thumbing though *Consumer Reports*.

"Hollywood's going nuts trying to figure out how to use it. It's going to be a big thing. Soon there's gonna be a TV show where you go around the corner to the 7-Eleven, and for ninety-nine dollars you'll rent some goggles and gloves. Mattel already has a game with a data glove where people can play simple games. . . . Right now there are several independent VR research groups designing systems. VR systems are being sold to architects, so they can model an entire building and walk through it to see where the problems might occur. VR is going to medical people as well."

It seemed from talking to my friends that virtual reality could transform every research, education and entertainment concept. Undoubtedly, from the moment its potential was uttered, people have been speculating on its erotic possibilities as well.

Howard Rheingold is the author of *Virtual Reality,* a primer on virtual evolution. He devoted one of his chapters to "teledildonics," literally the science of reaching out and touching someone. All Rheingold did in this chapter was to *speculate* on what erotic telepresence might be like, and he was deluged with calls from eager consumers who wanted to buy the perfect fucking machine.

"But why the obsession with a virtual sexual experience?" I asked him. "Real sex is a real possibility right now. A sexual experience is not like going to the moon. You could be playing out a sexual fantasy or taking a sexual risk right now, without any computer assistance, so what's the big deal? You'd think these people never had sex before!"

"Well, a lot of people don't have sex," Rheingold said. "A lot of people don't connect with other people. Most people believe sex is bad—c'mon, I don't have to tell you that. There is this tremendous reservoir of repressed force and good ole salacious interest. . . face it, the sex angle on anything sells. You have to look at the changing relationship that people feel, but can't quite articulate, between themselves and their bodies. There's some deep stuff going on here with our uneasiness about our future. And there's an unhappiness about our bodies that's been sold to us."

I pressed Howard about his pessimism. No one could write as charismatically as he does about the future and not have some high hopes.

He conceded a little. "Part of me has alarm bells about this artificial world that we're buying into, and part of me says you can't really judge the twenty-first century by twentieth century morality. What if there are twenty billion people on planet Earth? Do you really want them all to get in their cars and go somewhere? Maybe they should stay in their apartments and have very safe virtual sex with each other. Maybe that's a good thing.

"I thought the idea of a device which allowed you to communicate touch as well as visual and auditory representation was a neat idea," he went on. "Why not a communication device that includes body language? Body language includes dance and massage and sex."

Back at my coffee table, Richard Kadrey gave me a more detailed explanation of how a virtual sex experience would offer new points of view on human sexuality.

"If we go to some nice hotel to have sex, you still need

to provide your physical body, the physical body of the other person and the given surroundings. With VR, nothing in that scenario is locked in. Using VR there is no reason that you have to be you. You could look like anything and be any gender or combination of genders you want. There's no particular reason for you even to be a person. You could be the vibrator. You could be the bed or the TV at the end of the bed."

Finally, someone had given me a scenario that made me sit up and take notice. "You're right, I would love to be the vibrator—but that never would have occurred to me. Is everyone else as imaginative as you?" I asked him.

"No, no, ninety-nine percent of what's being desired is completely banal! VR has the potential to be every bit as banal as anything we've ever seen. It probably will be—at first. As in any kind of sex context, it's going to have the same development that pornography had; guys shooting loops of big dicks down in their basement and then a big come shot. I predict the first VR sex tool you'll find is a virtual blow job. The first programs are going to be real lame adolescent fantasies. Certainly you'll be able to buy some software that makes you look like Madonna. We'll probably see a lot of Tom Cruises and Rob Lowes wandering through VR."

Richard had just sprung the Pandora's Box I had been waiting to kick open. The computer business and the sexual entertainment industry are both classically male-dominated arenas. Were female desires and perspectives going to be alive in a virtual reality created by computer nerds? I have my own very feminine adolescent fantasies to attend to, and I don't imagine that they will be addressed by the mainstream of this business. Aside from equal opportunity self-indulgence, I wondered what kind of virtual software we could look forward to if it was going to be created by techies with no social skills or nurturing vision whatsoever.

My questions were leading me inevitably to the soul sister

of VR humanism, a woman named Brenda Laurel, a VR researcher and designer. Laurel is the co-founder of a VR development company called Telepresence. Everyone I had spoken to earlier repeated, "You need to meet Brenda. She's quite unusual in this business—she used to be an actress."

"Yes, I was in theater for years and years, until I had kids and couldn't make rehearsals anymore," Brenda remembers. "In 1976, I got involved in the computer game business. I learned from my bitter experiences there that what you do with a medium early on, and who gets access to shaping it, has a huge effect on the kind of messages and experiences that the medium is capable of supporting. I am active in getting artists involved in the beginning of VR so we end up with a medium that has a flexible range of applications and that has some kind of humanistic bias in it."

"What are the messages that you are so sick of?" I asked her.

"The computer game genre has grown an immune system with programmers utterly devoted to an adolescent male demographic and a very white, First World Western view of what's interesting to kids. The tragedy is that you are what you eat, and of course now the market only wants games about shooting and killing and blowing things up because it's the only choice that's ever been given to them."

"Well, what exactly is inherent in a masculine point of view so that men build new technology based on war games and infantile pornography?" I had to press her as to where she thought this testosterone technomania was coming from. Brenda apologized for making generalizations about men ("After all, I work with men who feel the same way I do"), but her criticism obviously contained more than a grain of truth.

"I know from fifteen years experience with computer guys that we have a class of people we call nerds who are radically uncomfortable with their bodies and their sexuality. I've had men tell me that one of the reasons they got into this business was to escape the social aspects of being a male in America—to escape women in particular. These are nice guys—not nasty, just shy, dweeby guys.

"When men talk about virtual reality," Brenda continued, "they often use phrases like 'out-of-body experience' and 'leaving the body.' These guys are not talking about out-of-body experiences in the way that some Eastern mystic or Peruvian Indian would. They are talking about it in the sense that if you slap a screen over your eyes you won't have to see air pollution. That is a Western industrial let's-dominate-the-earth kind of mentality.

"When women talk about VR they speak of taking the body with them into another world. The idea is to take these wonderful sense organs *with* us, not to leave our bodies humped over a keyboard while our brain zips off down some network. The body is not simply a container for this glorious intellect of ours."

I wondered how she planned to create a new humanist foundation. "Can you give me an example of something progressive you see happening in VR that indicates it won't suffer the same fate as the video arcade?"

"Okay, I'll give you an example that's half real, half fantasy. One thing about the adventure game genre is that you assume a character like a dwarf or a king, and sometimes you can choose your gender as well. Growing out of the adventure game business came a network called Habitat, developed by Lucasfilm in 1987. It's up and running in Japan. Instead of text on the screen you see graphics. You get to design a representation of yourself so that anybody else on the network sees a body and a face. It's very primitive, 2-D, kind of like Mr. Potato Head.

"The part that is fantasy," Brenda said, "is taking this notion into 3-D first-person network virtual reality systems. Sexuality is a huge part of self-concept, and in regular life we have a pretty limited palette. Our notions of clothing, make-up, hair style, and mannerisms are all very coded, with cast-in-stone notions of gender.

"What is possible in VR," she continued, "is that you can really broaden the palette of sexuality and therefore of gender. You could even be another species."

I blinked and remembered a deep desire that I hadn't thought about since I was young enough to play in a sandbox. "I would love to have a tail!"

"Oh yes, a prehensile tail would be very nice," said Brenda, "with lots of lovely fur."

Not all my initial reactions to VR were as playful as reinventing my dream body. VR constituted an instant invitation to bring my most forbidden taboos to life. I called up one of my erotic mentors, Honey Lee Cottrell. "How would you like to take the naughtiest thoughts you think about when you masturbate and program them into a virtual trip for the evening?" I asked, explaining the technology as graphically I could.

Her reaction took me aback. "It would never work," she said. "In my sexual imagination, I control my confrontation with the taboos in my fantasy. At certain points I jack up the volume, but then I can retreat from it. If I was forced to confront it full blast, I would just shut down. My taboo would close the wall of erotic response and I couldn't respond sexually."

Richard Kadrey was sympathetic to Honey Lee's reaction. "There seems to be a difficulty in differentiating fantasy life from real life. In your fantasy you're always somewhat aware that you're sitting on your couch. In VR, you wouldn't be aware of those details. The line between fantasy and reality would shift very quickly."

I had to press him further. "So, aside from our fear of running amuck in a virtual fantasy, what about social boundaries? Is it okay to have illegal or unethical sex in a virtual environment? In VR, you could presumably have sex with an animal, a close relative—you could even have sodomy in Georgia."

When I voiced this same speculation to Howard Rheingold, he replied, "Absolutely. And you will have these scenarios, as soon as the market will bear them. Just on the ordinary level, nothing kinky at all. Let's say you have a virtual 'office' with everyone in your office represented. You're pissed at your boss and you blow them all away. I'm sure millions of people will like to do that. If you're off your medication for the weekend or something. . . you might make a big mistake.

"That doesn't mean VR is automatically invalid," he continued, "just because it *could* be used that way. Nobody knows. I think a responsible thing to do would be to carefully look at whether VR can be designed to alter people's behavior. Wouldn't you rather know that?"

His question raised all my defenses. I don't want to believe that fantasies lead to literal reinactments. That's why I reject the thesis that porn "causes" violence. Is virtual reality going to do away with censorship, or will it make it stronger than ever? Will we soon be reduced to sitting around playing patty cake and singing "Mary Had a Little Lamb"? Will nothing controversial be allowed because strong feelings might lead to unacceptable acts? Richard counteracted my growing paranoia. "The same thing that might stop you from having a taboo experience in real life could also stop you in VR. If you have some taboo fantasy you want to play out, even if you create that fantasy exactly the way you imagine it in your head, it won't be anything like your fantasy and it won't be anything like real life. You'll be creating an altogether new kind of sexual experience."

The anticipation of an experience that was neither real nor fantasy, but *virtual*, made me wonder what was going to happen to the value of real life encounters. Many folks would already rather go to an adventure movie than go out and have a real adventure. The other possibility was that real life experiences would become rare and priceless. What would be the difference between experiencing childbirth and programming a virtual birth? Would you rather lose your virginity virtually or in reality? And what will be the future of beauty? If anyone can have perfect breasts and blonde hair down to the floor, will that be devalued as commonplace, or will we become the new virtual Aryan Nation? I found myself conjuring up the sweetest and most nightmarish possibilities to myself until I felt rather numb.

"Virtual realty today is about appearances," Brenda told me, "but ultimately it's got to be about behavior and interaction. Otherwise it would be so boring that people would just skip it. I mean, who wants to pay the price to run around like a paper doll?

"There is always something truly *me* in a VR scenario," Brenda said. Wasn't that what Perry had said about her fabulous faux phone sex personas?

Brenda spoke to me about her recent birthday. "I just turned forty. The older I get, the more I sense a growing divergence between who I am and who I'd like to be. Virtual reality is a demon that reinforces that schism. But it could also be a savior if it gives me a new arena in which to use my body, in ways that transcend its limitations."

Richard reminded me of what it's like to be on the brink of something we can hardly comprehend. "When man invented the camera, it was a mystical experience. The first time someone saw a photograph, it was like seeing God."

I thought about how my daughter squealed the first time she looked at a photograph and recognized herself. If we can bring our dreams to life—in a virtual landscape—it could be a vision of heaven, if not a little glimpse of hell. Hand me the goggles and glove.

UNDRESSING CAMILLE

I first met Camille Paglia, the most famous anti-lesbian feminist lesbian feminist in America, during my book tour for *Susie Sexpert's Lesbian Sex World*. I was speaking to a small attentive audience at Giovanni's Room bookstore in Philadelphia when suddenly this bag lady jumped out of her seat, and waving her arms as if she were hailing the last cab at Grand Central, yelled, "I am your *only* friend in academia."

I glanced meaningfully over at the bookstore employees. Security, *please!* But this woman was unstoppable. She came up and thrust a handful of papers in my direction—reviews of her new book. Later that night I unfolded them, expecting to read some cosmic conspiracy theory of the sort that are passed out every day in the Haight Ashbury. Instead I found *terribly* serious book reviews from the most highbrow quarters, commenting with great applause and alarm over this woman's grand oeuvre, *Sexual Personae*.

Very soon indeed, Camille Paglia was being quoted all over the American press on every sex-related subject from amateur porn videos to sexual harassment. I gleefully read her most sarcastic diatribes against the lesbian establishment, all the while thinking, Nobody in the straight world realizes she's exaggerating for effect.

In *Spin*, she called the battered women's movement a "motif." I recoiled and, at the same time, laughed with sheer black humor, recalling the way so many movements whose beginnings I've witnessed have gone on to take cynical and theoretical turns for the worse. Then, in *Esquire*, Paglia flatly declared lesbians to be sexually and intellectually "inert." Well, *you* haven't gotten any in a long time, I thought.

Camille, it turns out, is the first to agree. I talked to Paglia on the phone from a medieval village in France where I was holed up, writing the sequel to *Susie Sexpert*. I wish, though, that I had been able to interview her in the flesh. I would have had to tie her down to the bed to get candid responses to many of my questions.

Ruby Rich quoted Camille in the *Village Voice* saying, "Susie Bright and I are on the same track." It's true that we do have a few cars going in the same direction. But as much as she rails against academia, sometimes I think that Paglia has been locked in a tower of her own making for too long. How can she truly think that lesbians are the most "conformist" people on the face of the earth? Where was she during Operation Desert Storm? Has she never been to a suburban shopping mall? Her notions of men's brilliance in civilization-building and sexual vitality are often thought demeaning to women, but they're just as maddening for many men. Men, in her book, are incapable of intimacy or of a genuine emotional life. Perhaps the difference in our attitudes is simply one of—sexual personae. After all, Camille Paglia is a butch bottom, and Susie Bright is. . . not.

Susie Bright: You know, a lot of lesbians who read what you've written and your interviews are secretly laughing because they enjoy many of your criticisms. But when you call lesbians sexually inert, a lot of dykes say, "I'd love to throw Camille Paglia down on the floor and fuck her brains out."

Camille Paglia: Oh, I love it! Who are these women?

SB: You love it? (*Laughter.*) I could give you a list of people who have said this! Do you remember the night that I met you in Philadelphia?

CP: Of course, it's burned in my memory. (*Laughter.*)

SB: Well, it is in mine, too. You popped up like a jack-in-the-box, and you said that you were my only friend in academia. Why did you say that?

CP: You know, I'd heard about you, and then I decided to go see you when you spoke in Philadelphia. You started talking and I absolutely adored you. The way you were talking about sex was very humorous, spontaneous, improvisational. I am much more Amazon-like. I could see that since you are not in the academic world, you didn't understand the degree to which this absolutely sex-phobic, crazed, Moonie feminism has taken over the women studies programs. I'm so happy I do not have any of these amateurish, incompetent, resentful, angry women trifling with my brain.

SB: But about that night we met. . .

CP: The sexual revolution is not just about what you do with your body—it's about what you do with your mind— and that is what I thought was so great about your delivery. You picked up a coffee cup and outlined it to show where the G-spot was and you said to the girls in the room, "Now, this is a penis." The whole thing was so fabulous. Because you see, *comedy* is the secret. Humorlessness is a sign that someone is sick, and what we have got now in American feminism is humorlessness combined with sexual sanctimony and preaching. So, I saw your humor and I said: "This is it. Susie has art and is an artist. That is it. Exactly what is needed." So, that's why I popped up, and you had, of course, never heard of me because I was just barely on the scene—my book had just come out.

SB: No, I *had* heard of you, but I disagreed with you about women studies. I knew what you were talking about when you spoke about the feminist party line, but it's not unanimous. When I was in women studies programs in California, I'd have one class that would be very anti-porn, very fundamentalist feminist, and then I'd walk into another class and another women studies teacher—a lesbian—would be very sexually radical. My first exposure to S/M, butch/femme, etc., was on campus. And so when you said, "I'm your only friend in academia," I thought, Well, actually, you're not; there are lots of people who are very open-minded about this.

CP: But they're not making any impact! They are not the ones who are on TV talking about sex. This thing we just had on TV about Anita Hill and Clarence Thomas: All we saw were the most sexist, phobic idiots out there preaching. There was not one voice defending the right of someone to use sexual banter—and I refer to pornography—in our offices. Instead, the mention of pornography in a conversation was denounced as psychotic by people on that Senate committee, and no one—no one!—defended pornography in all those days.

The media discourse in America is being ruled by the most sex-phobic feminists. I am making headway because I am liberating people to say things that they have been saying only privately. Women must blame *themselves* for their impotence, their paralysis, their failure to engage in their own culture. It's no good being hip in a gay ghetto in a bar or some place. Feminism is damaging itself by its own prudery.

SB: What did you think when you saw your first issue of *On Our Backs?* How did you reconcile the kind of women you saw in the magazine with your view of lesbians as inert mother-sucking creatures? How did you feel when you opened up *On Our Backs* and everyone was fucking each other in the ass, talking dirty, cross-dressing and so on.

CP: First of all, you have to realize that I am playing a game. My remarks about lesbians are my form of guerrilla warfare. It is a criticism that comes from within, because for most of my life I have identified myself as a lesbian, so there is a lot of parody in what I'm saying. I was really excited when I first saw *On Our Backs*, but I also felt like it reflected a very minority culture from San Francisco, a culture that wasn't easily exported. All the S/M stuff for instance. . . . A friend—one of my ex-lovers—went to San Francisco, and I said to her, "Listen, there is this S/M scene there and it sounds exciting. What's going on?" And she said to me with great disgust, "I could be more S/M in a *dress*." (*Laughter*.) That's what she said.

I would be into S/M if I were very young. But as someone who grew up in the fifties, I have S/M in my *mind*. I think that the intensity of my S/M fantasies is such that seeing people really do it is sort of depressing to me. It's less than what I had created in my mind all these years when I was so frustrated for lack of meeting anyone with similar fantasies or attractions.

SB: Tell me one of your erotic fantasies: something that would be physically impossible or that you would never do, but that as a fantasy works beautifully.

CP: Well, this thing now with people strapping on dildos. Who said—I think it was Madonna—"I'm attracted to women, but basically I like to be fucked." And then she said, "Well, what about women strapping on a dildo?" And the interviewer said that there would be no point to it—it was a joke.

SB: Oh, that was Carrie Fisher.

CP: And she started laughing. And that is my problem with dildos. There is something slightly sordid about them, even though they are very attractive to me. If it came to it, I would try it, but the technology hadn't advanced yet when I was young, and now I think I'm beyond that. I think I'd feel . . . *absurd.* You know, if I was young, I could get into a whole line of scenarios. But now it's too late for me! I wrote this book that contains my fantasy life, and now I sort of look with bemusement at the rest of the world and I feel almost posthumous in certain ways.

SB: Really, you act like it's all over for you. These statements from you are a little bit hard to take.

CP: But it's true, Susie, it's true!

SB: But at this point there's got to be more than lack of opportunity to explain why you're not having this wild sex life. You're not going to be able to use that as an excuse.

CP: Well, at this point no, because there are star fuckers and groupies, obviously—so you cannot judge in terms of people's desire for me now what my life was like before this. But when I think about the past, I have to conclude that my level of intensity is really male. What lesbians did not like about me was my intensity. They really couldn't deal with it, whereas straight women—because they are used to dealing with men—never had a problem with me. It took me years and years and years before I saw this . . . . All I know is that I never connected with lesbians. I mean, I talk very fast, but even when I wasn't opening my mouth, something about me just was not interesting to lesbians. Men, on the other hand, have always been interested in me, but my problem with men is that I refuse to play any games of nursing and caretaking or do all the stroking you have to do to keep men going from day to day. What I want from men is good sex—virility.

SB: One thing I wonder as I read interviews with you is whether you had experienced anything similar to my own lesbian sex life. For years I had sex with women, and I was very inhibited because I thought what I wanted would be offensive coming from a feminist. I didn't want to be "like" a man; I didn't want to be unequal. All these things bothered me a lot, and looking back on it, it was just plain old inexperience and Catholic uptightness.

CP: I had the opposite problem in that I was trying to be dirty with women and I wasn't finding it. I was having a lot of trouble finding women who wanted just sex. My entire inability to relate to lesbians appears to be due to the fact that I was looking for sex—and they weren't. In the lesbian world you can't just walk into a bar. Oh no! You have to get into a sort of "musical chairs" group where you have to either play volleyball or do things with them or hang out with them.

SB: Isn't it like that any place else, though?

CP: Oh, no. That's certainly not the case with men's bars at all. The people arrive there as strangers looking for sex and it is absolutely admitted that the men are looking for sex—that has always been the case, and I find that so wonderful about men, that they don't even pretend that they are looking for friendship. It is a bold admission of desire.

SB: (*Laughter.*) Have you ever had what you would consider anonymous sex?

CP: Yes, but mostly with men. I was looking for it with women but I wasn't finding it. *That* is the story of my life—it's hilarious. I think that is my destiny—like the Ancient Mariner—to go through this wasteland and to suffer and then to write this book, so I accept what's happened to me. But I'm sure love will flourish, still. . . the love that always comes to people who are stars. That is not quite the same thing. One should not have to become an international star in order to get good sex, for heaven's sake!

SB: Was your first sexual experience with a man or with a woman?

CP: Let me think. Are you talking about *really* early? I think it was with boys. But then girls were later. I've been moving towards this idea of bisexuality because I have concluded that straight women are stronger than most lesbians. Last month, I was in Bloomingdale's and saw this incredibly butch woman, and I thought, Look at that woman, she is so fabulous! Wow! It turned out that she was a Jewish mother, and I realized the power emanating from her was coming from her control of men, and that was attracting me enormously: her power. And she was a complete being who controls the universe around her. I love it! That's what attracts me. But I rarely find that in lesbians. I rarely do. But listen, these women who want to throw me down on the floor—what coast are they on?

SB: Name your city, and I'll send one over. (*Laughter.*) You said that you've called yourself a lesbian most of your life, and yet you save your heaviest criticisms for lesbians. In some ways that makes sense because whatever group you identify with you also tend to be hardest on. But why were you attracted to women in the first place? Why did you call yourself a lesbian at all if you're so sickened by them that you never connected, nobody would talk to you, and you weren't on the softball team, yedy, yedy, yedy . . . .

Something had to make you feel passionate about women, and I think we all want to know what it is.

CP: When I began to be attracted to women, they weren't lesbians. I was basically attracted to the straight women of the world. That's what I'm attracted to. The point is, I identified myself as a lesbian before practically anyone.

SB: (*Laughter.*) Before Christ!

CP: What I mean is, I knew there were other lesbians, older ones, who were in the bars, and working-class lesbians in downtown Binghamton. When I was in college, I was dressing in gender-bending ways with ties, and I had

my hair short, even though I also had white and blue irides-
cent sixties eye make-up, you know? And I took a lot of
shit from very straight guys at the college. I wanted to find
a woman I could get along with, but the thing was, as
lesbian culture suddenly developed, it turned into this
feminist thing, and right from the start the feminist thing
was anti-art, anti-Freud, anti-this and anti-that, and suddenly I was not attracted to these women who were calling
themselves lesbians.

In the beginning I liked the old-style diesel dykes. I
thought they were great. They were women, older than me,
the ones in town, who were like men, and I got along with
them. They were funny, they were very competitive, they
would break beer bottles on the edge of a table and go for
people in the bar. . . . I thought they were great! Those
are the ones I got along with.

The new group of lesbian feminists really alienated me,
and so the only affairs I had were with people who did not
call themselves lesbians. There were a lot of straight women
who were borderline—had been with men—and they
somehow connected with me and got these crushes on me,
and they developed into major relationships.

For me, some of the greatest moments in lesbian eroticism have been in a heterosexual context. You know that
scene in *The Conformist* when Dominique Sanda is cares-
sing Stephanie Sandrelli's legs? It's absolutely *blazing* with
eroticism. I think lesbian sex lost big when it started to
think of itself as totally apart from the world of heterosexual sex. It lost a lot of the zap, the sizzle, and it degenerated
into what it is now, which is a huge, locked, insular cage.

SB: How come when men are together—completely without women—it doesn't turn into the same thing?

CP: Well, sex is often a longing for intimacy. Women have
this ability to be intimate without getting into bed with
each other, this intuitive understanding of each other and

people in general, and that leads to this fusion phenomenon in lesbian relationships. But men aren't *capable* of being intimate. Ultimately they are blocked from their own emotions. There are some exceptions—artists, some gay men—but most heterosexual men really don't have a clue about what is going on in their own emotional lives. So when men have sex, that desire to have sex with another man is a desire for intimacy which has no other way to express itself. I'm not for intimacy, particularly. I think we have *too much* intimacy right now.

SB: (*Laughter.*) Camille, do you really have too much intimacy in your own life?

CP: No, but I think there is too much intimacy in the world. Sex is hottest for me, usually, in the beginning, when people don't really know each other. And then the minute you start knowing someone, it just gets into this immediate banal thing—"Okay, who's going to take the shower first?. . . Your mother's on the phone." I grew up in the fifties. I spent my whole life *rebelling* against banality!

SB: Camille, who do you tell your secrets to?

CP: Who do I tell my secrets to?

SB: A woman or a man.

CP: Well, I'm particularly close to women. I mean, secrets? What kind of secrets? Either gay men or women. Why?

SB: Well, we are talking about intimacy. I don't buy it when you say that there is too much intimacy. I know what you're saying about the hunt being over, and all you can think about is TV dinners, but that is not intimacy, either. Intimacy and sexual excitement together is incredibly intoxicating, don't you think?

CP: Well, one of my ex-lovers went back to being straight, and of course all the lesbians turned on her and said:

"How can you betray us? You were the greatest lesbian in the world. . . ." After a while in lesbian relationships, she got tired of the need to know every thought, to share everything. It was just too much.

The thing about men that is so refreshing is that you just sort of pat them on the head and they go off and conquer the North Pole. Basically, they are slightly absurd and you get great sex from them and so forth, but that intricate fusion of the mental lives is possible only between women and it eventually suffocates the sex—it certainly does for me. Men and women have hot sex because they will never know each other. Men can never truly bond in the way that women can.

I am sick and tired of women retreating to their own world. They've got to join the human race and change the culture without whining about it, about Big, Bad Daddy Patriarchy. That is so simplistic, so adolescent, so naïve. And that is why I am going on the attack. American sexuality is always puritanical, but in the lesbian world everyone is so damned smug and self-satisfied, always patting each other on the back, all so complacent: "Oh, we're so fabulous." No, they aren't! Maybe there are pockets that are "so fabulous," but I haven't been able to find them, and I've been looking for twenty damn years. Look at Jodie Foster, the big feminist, always preaching and sermonizing on her pulpit, but does she have the slightest guts to say anything about her bisexuality or lesbianism or whatever it is? No guts! How about Lily Tomlin? Constant feminist preaching. No guts whatsoever! We've got to get something going here.

SB: There's a difference between criticizing these celebrities' lack of courage and damning all lesbians as regressive. When you do that there is nobody, Camille, left to defy, as *lesbians*. There's not you, there's not me, there's not the women who want to throw you on the floor and fuck you until you're blind. There's *no one* left!

CP: They don't exist anymore because they've all become these pathetic little victims. Sleeping with women is fabulous, and I am just trying to move it outward. I want women to be with women who are straight, who do not close themselves down against male lust.

Women, I think, are naturally bisexual. You know I'm not telling lesbians to stop sleeping only with women, but to leave open a part of the brain toward men and accept male lust and find men extremely attractive and get horny in relation to men and ogle their bodies and do something with them. Then sex with women will be hotter.

SB: I have a different take on you, Camille, a different label for you: I think that you are a "butch bottom." I think you are very attracted to fem women who might flip you. Virile men you admire, but you can't be in love with them. You are also very competitive with other lesbians who you sense are butch but not as butch as you or as good as you, which is typical among butch dykes: They don't like each other or have sex with each other very often, and they compete for the same girls, and most of them are "butch bottoms," and they would agree with a lot of what you say. When you talk about the bad stuff, the banal stuff that we see, and even the latest Nyack Press romance literature, I understand—and every lesbian understands—what you are talking about. . . . But when you say you see *On Our Backs* and San Francisco as a kind of minority, unusual experience—it isn't, it isn't! The very fact that you are discussed and a controversy in the way that you are in the lesbian world today has something to do with the fact that you have forerunners. You can say, "Oh, Susie Bright is on the same track as I am even though she is in a different world than I am," because you're *not* the only one. You really aren't. There are a lot of dykes out there who are thrilled to hear some of the things you are saying but can't go up and shake your hand because you are damning the whole group. You call it a guerrilla tactic but there is guerrilla with a "u" and gorilla with an "o."

CP: (*Laughter.*) But I'm trying to break into these bunkers of women studies, of feminism, of lesbian feminism, and so on—they're absolutely locked tight, and what I am doing is blowing them all open. I just *am*. People who were invisible are actually talking to each other or yelling at me for the first time. And there is also an element of revenge in it—no doubt about that—because I am pissed that I spent the best years of my sex life in misery.

SB: What was the last straw? Nobody had a ball and chain tied to you all those years, so there must have been something about lesbian sex that you liked. . . but finally something happened that really turned your heel and I want to know what that was.

CP: All those decades of frustration. . . . there were a few periods when I was with someone, but mostly it was an incredible amount of frustration: going to places and trying to meet people and just not getting anywhere at all. *Nowhere!* Even when I thought, Oh, this one seems interesting, she would turn out to be so disconnected. So, I decided I would destroy the present structure by ridiculing it and confederating it and using the spotlight of my attention—bringing that spotlight to problems people may talk about privately, but don't dare to say publicly. And by the way, this is the same technique I am using in terms of academia—*the same thing*. The point is, if *my* life has been miserable, there are a lot of other women whose lives have been miserable, too.

SB: What do you think of my take on your sexuality?

CP: I thought that was fabulous! I loved that.

SB: Oh, really?

CP: Yes, I don't know if it's true, but it gives me a nice little "free feel."

SB: How do you feel when people call you a fag hag? Does that upset you, or do you laugh and think, god, that's really true.

CP: Well, I certainly love that phrase. Some of my most intimate relationships have been with gay men. I have been profoundly influenced by gay men. The way they value their beauty and art and their interest in pornography, the level of their sexual desire, their elitism. . . . I believe in the elitism of talent. I can't bear the egalitarianism in feminism: Heaven forbid we should make any qualitative judgments about anything.

SB: If you had a cock for a week, what would you do with it?

CP: Well, I would have liked one twenty or even thirty years ago. I think there was a period when I felt that would have solved all my problems because the women I was interested in tended to be straight. Now it would be a pain in the ass—having that thing in there all the time. That's my attitude.

SB: You have talked about the idea of victimization in modern feminism, and yet in this conversation you've referred to yourself as being, sexually and socially, a complete loser.

CP: No, *maladjusted*. A loser is someone who is depressive and passive. I was always an activist. I was a rebel and I was burning with anger from the start. I'm saying that conflict and combat and angst and anguish all lead, eventually, to great achievement. And they have certainly done so in the figures that I admire—someone like Michelangelo, the turbulence in his character. What I don't like in the lesbian world is that it is so damn cozy.

SB: Are your parents alive?

CP: Well, my father just died earlier this year after two years of being ill. My mother is alive, yes.

SB: So, what did they think of the book?

CP: Well, I wouldn't say either of them has read it, but my father read some of it. He was a professor.

SB: Was he surprised how famous you are?

CP: Famous? I'm famous, but I'm not *that* famous. I'm not a household word—yet. (*Laughter.*)

SB: You are in my household.

CP: Yes, I'm a *Cosmo* girl now. Listen, I was in Boston two nights ago, and a woman from Russia plopped down this magazine for me to autograph. I'm on the cover of a magazine in Russia! I said, "What the hell is this?" It was a reprint of my *Playboy* interview, and they illustrated it with pictures of a streetwalker from Kiev, which I loved, and I thought, My god, there are streetwalkers in Kiev that now know that I, Camille Paglia, support them in all prostitution! They had reprints of other articles about me from Japan, Taiwan, Holland, Brazil, Portugal, Australia—you name it! What's happening is like a *world phenomenon!* What I'm doing is putting the idea of women as intellectuals back on the map. . . . What more can I say? I am a *real* feminist.

SB: But it gets to the point where someone reads what you are saying—for instance, about masculinity signifying sexual freedom and that women will have to be willing to accept certain risks like date rape if they want this freedom—and thinks, That's right. Women should wear veils. Women should not go out at night because they are not prepared to handle sexual freedom.

CP: Now, you can't believe that I have to be responsible for people misreading what I am saying and having half-baked ideas about me! I am a new thinker; I have just come on the scene, and I have *the* most comprehensive vision of sexuality in the world right now. . . . As for myself, I feel like I'm a sexual freak—my life in that area has been kind of miserable. And yet I got the compensation of writing this completely pornographic, massive book which eroticizes everything in history, and now the book is seducing other people, too! The *book* seduces people for me.

SEX AND THE SINGLE PEST

I was in Europe when our newest Supreme Court Justice—then a mere nominee—was accused of sexual harassment. Professor Anita Hill, his aide for three years, testified to the Senate confirmation committee that her boss had continuously degraded her with his sexual come-ons and remarks. The Senators in turn questioned both Hill's credibility and Thomas' culpability by getting Deep Inside every glistening detail of Hill's allegations.

I spoke to my friend Pat in Michigan from France the weekend of the most salacious testimony. "Can't we close the curtains?" she said, when I told her the hearings were top headline news all over the world. "I can't stand the whole universe watching these peckerwoods. How can anyone respect us?"

Respect? Well, international bullies command some sort of respect, however obsequious. Western Europe reported on the hearings with as straight a face as it could, while clearly insinuating that the United States is in the grips of a sexual psychosis. Yes indeed.

The BBC reported the news with as much stomach as it has for anything sexual. "In Britain, sex pests are not illegal," the anchorman reminded viewers. "But *should* they be? Or is it a further infringement of the rights of the individual?"

"Sex pests"—I rather liked that nickname. It suggested that better than a law would be some sort of roach spray that you could squirt in the offender's loathsome face. "Pest Be Gone!" you'd shout with a squirt, and Peeping Thomas would fizzle away like mildew in the shower.

My feminist fantasy was not included in the approach that the European news community took to the proceedings. A French government official said that this oddity, sexual harassment, would never happen France because, "Our men are so seductive, there is no need to harass." Of course this sort of chauvinism is often just another part of the sex pest's M.O.—he thinks he's seductive; you think he's a roaring jerk.

Harassment doesn't reveal itself in a mere proposition— it's in the strings attached, in the refusal to take "no" for an answer. Take the sexual titillation out of it, and it stands as a bald issue of consent, of freedom from coercion. But this is exactly the point that sexual liberation turns on. Can you do what you please without oppressing anyone else? Feminists have been arguing that one for a couple of decades now, and moral righteousness has more often than not upstaged sexual education or tolerance.

Looking at the Thomas/Hill controversy as an issue of sexual freedom helped me distinguish between how much Americans care about harassment and how much we care about sexual taboos. The Senate committee found Thomas innocent of being a sex pest, but more importantly, they found him to be sexually innocent and therefore judicially sound.

Did he or didn't he hound her? There was no authentic debate on that count. Despite all the counter-witnesses and interrogation, it doesn't matter what Hill's ulterior motives may have been. Every woman who watched her testimony knows from personal experience exactly what she was talking about. American women have had it up to *here* with getting ahead through sexual humiliation. This won't be the end of it.

But I'm hardly the only one to comment on the double standard at work in the One Patriarchy Under God. What interests me more acutely is that in order for Thomas to be confirmed, he had to be cleared, not so much as a menace or a badger, but as a sexual, African American, full-grown man. He had to be declared sexually CLEAN, his whites whiter, his brights brighter. A man can be hired for any position in America despite being an arrogant pest; in fact, that might be considered an asset in some fields. But it is impossible to hold any legal job in the Untied (sic) States, let alone the grandest one of all, and be openly sexual. And this is why some people wisely say that whores hold the only honest jobs in the land.

If Anita Hill had testified that Thomas had approached her with a box of chocolates and a straightforward proposition to go to bed—plus the insinuation that her job depended on accepting his offer—it would have been sexual harassment. But that story would NOT have blown the TV ratings out of weekend sports. Though perhaps an adequate candidate for feminist debate, the hearings would not have galvanized the entire half-dead feminist leadership into raging tigers.

What made Hill's testimony tick like a bomb were the excruciating racial and sexual taboos it revealed for all to squirm and sweat over. My god, thirty years of liberal insistence that we stop judging black men by the size of their penises just fell apart on a Saturday afternoon. Pornographic fuck films? Isn't that something homo, rape-o, white perverts prefer? Isn't that what our Attorney General has dedicated this country's police forces to wiping out? Isn't that what Pee Wee did? Did anyone do a conspiracy cross-check to see if Thomas and Pee Wee saw the same flicks?

If someone had the honesty to truly look at sex in this country, he or she would find Clarence Thomas's tastes and comments utterly banal. Long Dong Silver is a name known to anyone who has had the slightest brush with dirty movies. I was only a teensy bit surprised when my coal delivery man in my small French village (population two hundred) told me about the Long Dong movie *he* had seen.

Really, the Coca-Cola episode was the topper. Any regular American Coke drinker who hasn't by the age of sixty found a pubic hair somewhere near or on his or her aluminum can has been living in a bubble. That's the way it is with hair. It floats around and sticks on things. Who was shocked by this story? Ten-year-olds? The public laughed their heads off, but the state insisted that the emperor still wore his clothes.

The Senate committee members, whichever side they were on, had neither a sense of humor nor a sense of history. To the genuine alarm of the women's movement, the committee also failed to see Thomas's behavior as a feminist issue—they saw it as a sleazebag issue. Or rather these men think that feminism *is* defending women against sleazebags.

Unfortunately, most of the feminist establishment also thinks that the crux of feminism is defending women against gross sex. Did feminist Catherine MacKinnon go on the tube to say that Clarence Thomas could have a ball reading skin mags on his own time, but not on Anita Hill's? No, she went for the classic one-two punch: Men are evil, and pornography (say this word as if you are strangling) makes them this way. Some call this approach radical feminism, but I call it nineteenth century protectionism. Take my Carry Nation, please.

You know, if Clarence had got up and said—don't laugh!—"I really do love watching and talking about sex, and Long Dong is my cocksman hero—but I would never bring this up to embarrass or intimidate an employee," I would have believed him. Because to admit that he was sexual would have cost him the Supreme job forever. If he had only admitted to harassing Hill, they would have forgiven him. You know they would.

In the end, it was the Senate's disgust and shame about the whole sexiness of the issue that made them do the most typical thing of all: Deny it. The Senators dared you to look at Clarence Thomas and his unbelievable wife with their pained, pinched faces and try to imagine them having sex, talking about sex, or watching a blue movie. Hard to believe? Yes, and your parents never had sex either.

Remember the Meese Commission? It was a 1986 government-sponsored hyster-inquiry about the effects of pornography. They found many witnesses to sit in silhouette behind blinds and tearfully tell how reading *Penthouse* led to drugs, white slavery and bulimia. How incredible that they didn't have one token witness, not even with a bag over her head, who could say, "Gee, my husband and I watched *The Devil in Miss Jones* and we had hot sex and a great talk about the lunacy of Catholicism afterwards." The Commission could not even produce one average soul to file an affidavit saying that she had looked at plenty of skin magazines over the years, and nothing came of it. . . nothing at all. She moved to the suburbs and sold aluminum siding. One day she found a pubic hair in her Coke and wondered how it got there.

Admitting that one is sexual doesn't mean making a nuisance out of oneself. It doesn't mean being a pig. There is actually a way to acknowledge one's sexuality without getting in anybody else's face about it.

Of course, for many Americans, to know others are sexual *is* to be offended. This is exactly what the homophobes have cried about for ages: They don't want to know you're gay on the job, because it's blatant, it's obnoxious.

What about women in blue collar jobs who complain that the guys have cheesecake pictures adorning their lockers? Dear Abby recently ran a fabulous go-round about this in the daily paper. A woman worker might call pin-ups a perfect example of sexual harassment, but it could also be true that she's perfectly embarrassed by knowing, up front, that her co-workers think about women in a sexual manner. It might make her feel threatened or resentful. Or she might blow their minds and put up her own beefcake. They'll be more spooked by her sexuality than she is by theirs.

What's good for the gander is a whole 'nother world for the goose. It's typical for men to display their sexual interests, and it's typical for women to feel ostracized and objectified by their display. But neither is "natural" or particularly honest. Do most men hang pictures of what really turns them on, of their most personal fantasies? Half of them tolerate the babe in the calendar because of the Harley pictured underneath her. Do women look at those pictures and think about what they mean to that man, or do they compare themselves to Miss Tool and Die and want to die themselves? The best response in Dear Abby was from the gal who put up her own female soft-core poster and enjoyed the hell out of herself, checking out which co-workers were admiring and which were homophobic or appalled.

She had a lot of nerve. Whether she knows or not, she not only showed her sexual preference, but she showed the men she was checking out theirs. All the tits were on the wall.

For women, straight or gay, to acknowledge their sexuality on the job is seen as "asking for it." For Anita Hill and others like her, just being the *object*, not the instigator, of sexual indiscretion made her wonder if she was doing something wrong.

Women are constantly reacting to men's perception of our desirability and our sexual potential, yet we rarely get there first. If we declare our sexuality up front, not as pests, but as full-blooded adult women, we not only risk being excluded from the upwardly mobile ladder path that Clarence Thomas so studiously followed, but we risk losing what little security we've already attained.

A man who admits his lust is seen as a foolish, unambitious stud, but a lusty woman is a fallen woman, a whore. Sexual women lose the protection of the double standard. But is it so awful to lose our end of a bad bargain? Where do fallen whores go, anyway? I'd like to see one go straight to the top, the Supreme Court bench. We gotta have someone we can trust.

MEN WHO LOVE LESBIANS
(Who Don't Care for Them
Too Much)

When the first lesbian-produced erotica came out in the mid-eighties, one question was repeated over and over on the cosmic lesbian feminist P.A. system. Just like your junior high school principal summoning the usual suspects to his office, this voice of authority demanded: Will this new lesbian porn be sold where men can buy it?

Like so many almost-sexual questions, the query says more about the questioners—lesbians—than it does about men; in this case, both subjects are worth investigating. Why do lesbians care if men see their sexuality? Why do men want to see it?

Let's clear the air by asking the *real* question right off the bat. Lesbians want to know what men will *do* when they look at pictures of lesbians getting it on. Will they grab their dicks, get hard, and have explosive orgasms on the page? Will they create their own androcentric finale to the visual fantasy before them? Will they pull the two dykes apart and "give them what they're really asking for"?

I've received many letters about lesbian sex from men, and photographs. They send me pictures of lesbians they have known and/or loved, pictures of themselves nude and in women's clothes, torn pages from old sixties lesbo pornography which they compare to current lesbian erotica, and copies of my articles with the parts they like best underlined. Their discussions range from the most pornographic and perverse to the most sentimental. One guy sent a toy bunny for my newborn daughter, along with a picture of himself looking rather ingratiating in a French maid's outfit. Could he do my ironing while I was getting back my strength?

I feel like I know why men are turned on to lesbian sex. Their reactions, though taboo, are neither as monstrous as lesbians imagine nor as sissified as "straighter" men believe. I'm certain I heard from the hard-core, not the guy who looks at the annual blonde twin pictorial in *Playboy* and says, "Nice tits." But even the man who shows only a passing interest in a soft-focus lesbian photo spread reveals traces of the classic dyke daddy persona: The lesbian-identified man.

Most men who like this kind of erotica don't want to *save* the lesbians, they want to *be* the lesbians. Lesbian lovemaking is soft and slippery and it never, ever ends. There's no hard-on to worry about, and one orgasm leads to the next, sometimes fast and furious, sometimes gentle as a breath. It combines feminine intimacy with multiple climaxes, and in those notorious group sex scenes, there are more nice pairs of tits than you can count. Who doesn't want to be a lesbian if that's what you get to do all day?

And lesbians are free. In the lesbian fantasy world, dykes are Amazons. They don't need men and they don't have time for any bullshit. They are disgusted with the male gender—and why shouldn't they be? Lesbians *are* superior. Most men are disgusted with other men, too, so this isn't such an awful idea to them. Every time I get a letter from a man who lauds lesbian superiority, I can guess how competitive he is with his fellow men.

Dyke daddies don't know each other. Despite my call for a convention, CR group, or a night out on the town, their whole *raison d'être* depends on not identifying with similar men. Very butch of them.

My most faithful dyke daddy pen pal is Luke, who lives in Port Arthur, Texas, Janis Joplin's hometown. He is sixty-five. He told me the story of his teen years, when every sexual expression *except* intercourse was possible before marriage. His first sexual experience was putting his fingers in a woman's pussy. She came that way. Finger fucking and cunnilingus remain his favorite sexual activities to this day. Coitus is at the bottom of the list. His vicarious pleasure in a woman's genital sensation is so acute that he connects it to his own cock. Luke is another version of guys who say, "I can't come until you do." They aren't being chivalrous; it's the truth.

I listened sympathetically to Luke's adolescent sex history. Most of us have sexual experiences during budding pubescence that stay with us for the rest of our lives. Unfortunately, early puberty is also when commercial pornographic images of lesbian sex begin and end. In mainstream erotic fantasies, lesbian sex never grows up; it's a female Peter Pan on a loop. I understand that for some, lesbian romanticism can be an escape from the adult world, but that isn't much of a thrill for grown-up dykes. Until lesbians began making their own erotica, there didn't seem to be any pictures of women over eighteen making love to each other.

Luke has sent me some photos and drawings he has made of the lesbians he admires. They are not teens, and they do not look like porn models. One of them has uncombed hair and sports a "Women Take Back the Night" t-shirt. Another is more butchy, with a crew cut, but a very womanly figure. They both look tough as nails. I guess you'd have to be, being queer in rural Texas.

Luke has had awkward and rare sexual experiences with both these women. Occasionally, he gives money to one of them. I suppose the other woman is aware of his fantasy-driven devotion, since he does something very unlesbian-like: he keeps propositioning her. She keeps turning him down. . . until one day, she says, "Oh Christ, I'll give you a hand job as a friend, and that's the end of it." Or maybe

95

she just wants to get fucked sometimes without all the bother of niceties afterwards. So lesbians, too, can be very unlesbian-like, very improper by pious community standards that good little dykes are supposed to live by. I could line up women from here to Siberia who have searched for and, when they could, have taken advantage of sex without attachments. Many of them would be lapsed-monogamy lesbians.

Luke is married to an ex-dyke, or so he tells me. She has participated in more than one *ménage* with him. I love thinking about these two senior citizens, retired now and roaming the country in their Winnebago. You'll never read about them in the American Association of Retired Persons newsletter.

Perhaps I have the bizarre privilege of being acquainted with the fringe of America, but I think dyke daddies are quite common. If lesbianism is so perverse (God forbid your daughter should be one . . .), then why is lesbian eroticism apparent in every sort of art and entertainment? The lesbian aesthetic, in music videos and fashion magazines, not to mention vampire movies, portrays all the sensuality, female yearning and mystery that can't be expressed by any conventional heterosexual love story. The love that dare not speak its name is actually shouting out loud.

So why are lesbians offended by male attention? There are many reasons. I'd like to dispense with most ridiculous, albeit popular, one first. There are many people, men and women, gay and straight, who base their sexual preferences on extreme revulsion to bodily fluids. In lesbian quarters, these women are outraged at the prospect of men picking up lesbian porn and presumably ejaculating all over pages 46-47. The thing that really galls these women is the cum itself. They have more in common with do-it-in-the-dark straight men and women who won't give each other head than they do with any tradition of Sapphic purity. I was so pleased when female ejaculation began getting some publicity; now, I thought, all those wet-phobic fanatics won't be able to wrap the holy cloak of feminism around themselves. Women spray the sheets, too.

But putting the matter of warm liquids aside, there are far more complicated reasons why lesbians don't like the spotlight on their sexuality.

The prime political slogan of lesbian liberation has been to demand visibility, to be seen as a LESBIAN population, not to be swept into the homo-stack with gay men. But feminine discretion and caution inform a great deal of the lesbian world that is not anxious to make their sexuality a feature of that visibility. Their lesbianism is as much about keeping their private lives out of the private eye as it is about anything else. The person who first said "I wish they weren't so blatant" was probably such a dyke.

What Ms. Mind-My-Own-Business hates more than anything is a portrait of herself that includes the sexual. She fears that if she proclaims her sexual desire she will risk losing credibility and authority in the real world. Like any lesbian, she despises male condescension, so much so that she would rather be treated like a nun than a little girl. Sure, she'll fight rather than switch, but what she'd really rather do is avoid a confrontation in the first place. Unfortunately, her desires for privacy and discretion are so complementary to the stigma against homosexuality that the closet is always going to provide her best immediate comfort.

Many dykes have rejected the closet because of their tremendous pride and enthusiasm about lesbian culture: the music, the literature, the festivals. But some of these otherwise outspoken women feel that explicit lesbian erotica detracts from and even degrades the "higher purpose" of lesbian life. The tradition of separating art from sex, politics from sex, and romance from sex is clearly bigger than the lesbian community; it is generated by the same puritan standard that divorces our bodies from our minds.

I once had a argument with a woman who was upset to see a magazine like *On Our Backs* for sale in a regular bookshop. At first I told her that regular bookstores are where you find lesbians. They don't just check into some dyke commissary to get their daily requirements. But all she could talk about was men ripping off our energy when they buy lesbian erotica.

I asked her, "Do you hear about gay men feeling drained because some straight person bought a copy of the *Advocate*?"

"Well, that's not the same," she said. "They're stronger."

Exactly.

The arrival of lesbian erotica provided the most defiantly tangible evidence of a dramatically changing lesbian generation. Can men buy it? Yes, and straight women too, and gay men who don't know the first thing about lesbianism. Lesbian erotic images have changed the face of popular sexual knowledge, because dyke pioneers have completely enlarged the discussion of female sexuality. Lesbian erotica has shown us what our bodies look like, the range of our sexual emotions, and the explicit details of how we make love.

Lesbians *are* visibly sexual in a public manner that was unseen even ten years ago. It's been years since I've heard anyone wonder out loud what two women could possibly do together in bed. Folks know better. We *are* stronger.

EGG SEX

In 1966, when I was eight years old, my mother gave me a little pink book, *A Baby is Born*. In great detail, and with lots of close-ups and diagrams, it described exactly what a sperm and egg looked like and how they joined together, with subsequent portraits of the developing fetus.

How did the sperm meet the egg to begin with? The book said simply, "Mommy and Daddy love each other very much. They lie close together and, after performing intercourse, the sperm is on its way to fertilize the egg." There was no accompanying diagram, so I made what was probably my first earnest attempt to read between the lines of any piece of literature. I gleaned nothing.

Twenty-five years later, I was pregnant, and this time I went out and bought my own collection of pink and blue books bulging with instruction for prospective parents. Of course, there was a great deal to learn about fetal development and breast-feeding techniques, but I couldn't help but check each index under "Sexuality—during and after pregnancy." All the manuals, from Dr. Spock to the latest yuppie know-how, followed an almost identical script: "Mommy and Daddy love each other very much. . . ." Following this vein, the paragraphs on sexuality gave advice that was inexplicit, vague, and almost threatening in their avoidance of the nitty-gritty.

Steeped in a romance-novel notion of marriage, sexual advice to pregnant moms, whether revealed in print or in the strange silences at the doctor's office, gives short shrift to the dramatic changes in women's sexual physiology and desires. Great emphasis is placed on how to cope with the ambivalent husband's feelings towards his wife's body and the burden pregnancy puts on their normal sexual routine.

None of these books was written in the sixties. All of them glow with feminist and holistic approaches to mothering, supporting working moms, refuting the sexist prejudices against breast-feeding, and offering all manner of enlightened positive self-esteem for the mother-to-be. I began to wonder if anyone *knew* what went on in women's sexual lives during pregnancy. The most definitive statement the books managed was: Sometimes she's hot, sometimes she's not. This wouldn't be the first time that traditional medicine had nothing to contribute to an understanding of female sexuality.

Meanwhile, my clit started to grow. Everyone knows that a pregnant woman's breasts swell in accompaniment to her belly, but why had no one told me that my genitals would also grow? My vulva engorged with blood; my labia grew fatter; my clit pushed slightly out of its hood. I was reading absolutely everything on the subject of pregnant sex by this point and, by picking out the fragments of pertinent information, I learned I was not peculiar in this regard.

It's a little embarrassing to be thirty-one years old and finally get the message that my primary and secondary sexual characteristics are not simply for display and petting. I was being physically and psychologically dominated by the life growing inside me, and of course I wanted both to escape and to submit. I was unusually sensual and amorous, and yet, twenty weeks into pregnancy, I found I could not successfully masturbate the way I had been doing since I was a kid. I was stunned and a little panicky. My engorged clitoris was different under my fingers; too sensitive to touch my usual way, and what other way was there?

That's when it hit me. The experts all say that it is a mystery why some women get more horny when they're pregnant while others lose interest. I'll tell you something—no one loses interest. What happens is that your normal sexual patterns don't work the same way anymore. Unless you and your lover make the transition to new ways of getting excited and reaching orgasm, you are going to be very depressed about sex and start avoiding it all together.

It's not just a technique change, either. Feeling both desirable *and* protected are essential to a pregnant woman, and if protection is not forthcoming from the outside, she will build a fortress that cannot be penetrated.

I no longer believe that some women don't feel sexual during those long nine months. Some are frightened by the sexual changes their growing bodies demand. But so many others confided to me, "I was so hot, and I couldn't explain it to just anyone."

It's an awesome feat of American puritanism to convince us that sex and pregnancy do not mix. It's the ultimate virgin/whore distinction. For those nine months, please don't mention how we got this way—we're Mary now.

Your average Mary's physical transformation is quite different from an immaculate conception. A woman's vagina changes when she is pregnant, much like her vulva and clit. The lubrication increases; its smell and texture are different. Often exhibiting a pregnancy-type yeast infection, her genitals smell like a big cookie.

When I fucked during my pregnancy, I felt like I was participating in a slow elastic taffy pull. I was more passive sexually than ever before, with no ambition to strap one on, or get on top, or do much of anything besides take it all in and float. I was one gigantic egg cozy.

Truthfully, you don't get gigantic for at least five or six months. The advice books make much controversy over positions for intercourse, but I didn't find positioning to be that big a deal. It's typical of mainstream sex books to focus on "positions" in the masculine way one might prepare a sports manual. You can fuck on your back for a long time if you like, as long as your partner doesn't insist on collapsing upon you. Flat on one's belly is of course impossible after six months, but slightly turned to the side works just fine. It is often recommended that the woman get on top, but as I said, I couldn't be bothered.

Sex is also a crucial way to prepare for childbirth. Start with the premise that birth is the biggest sex act you will ever take part in, and everything will flow from that. If you are smart and take childbirth preparation classes, you may even get a teacher who knows something about the sexual side of birth.

My teacher was very subtle. She gave us an almost unreadable handout in the fourth month, an instruction sheet for an exercise called "perineal massage." I thought of my perineum, the little inch of skin running between my vagina and my anus. How could rubbing something the size of a birthday candle help me in labor?

The flyer (which opened, of course, with the obligatory spiel: "Mommy and Daddy love each other very much. . .") said that Daddy should massage and finger the vaginal opening until he could put more and more of his fingers inside, relaxing the vaginal muscles through such caresses until he might be able to press a small orange or even his whole hand into Mommy's opening.

His whole hand! I called up one of my friends who has the breadth of experience as both a mother of two and a retired porn star. "Is 'perineal massage' really fist fucking?" I asked her.

"Of course," she said, laughing, "and it really helps."

I could see why immediately. A hand going inside my pussy is a little like a baby's head trying to move outside into the world. How exciting! For the first time I felt a surge of confidence about my chances for a successful labor. Since I had practiced fisting, clearly I was in great shape for the real thing.

Perineal massage is not discussed in every hospital or prenatal setting. Most couples and their care providers are steeped in the dominance of penis-vagina intercourse. It requires a different sort of orientation to devote attention to the possibilities of fingers and hands. But with a little encouragement and a flyer with pictures and plain English, I think more parents would enjoy the intense relaxation and vulnerability that comes with fisting, or "oranging," if you prefer.

I pestered my teacher for three weeks about whether she thought using a vibrator during labor would be helpful for pain relief. She said each time that we would discuss it next week. She recommended all sorts of other distractions and exercises: going to the bathroom frequently, changing positions, getting in the bathtub, focusing on a special object, etc. Well, I decided on my own that my Hitachi magic wand was going to be my focus object. I believed that stimulating my clit would be a nice counterpoint to the contractions going on inside my belly.

I have a great photograph of me in the delivery room, dilated to six centimeters, with a blissful look on my face and my vibrator nestled against my pubic bone. I had no thought of climaxing, but the pleasure of the rhythm on my clit was like sweet icing on top of the deep, thick contractions in my womb. I would have been too tired and distracted to touch myself with my fingers at that point, and the power cord was just one of about ten that the doctors had coming from my bed. Due to my baby's unusual breech position, I had a complicated birth that finally ended in an emergency Cesarean. But I had a great labor.

My friend Barbara confessed to me after her first child that she had never been so turned on in her life. When the baby's head was crowning, she called out to her husband over and over, "I want to come, touch me, please touch me!"—and he thought she was hysterical.

We are utterly unaccustomed to seeing birthing as a sexual experience. A lot of us think of childbirth as something close to death; at least, that's what I was afraid of.

I heard women screaming in the rooms next to me at the hospital and I knew those screams weren't exclusively from physical pain, but from wild, wild fear. It's terribly frightening when you don't know what your body is doing and when your sexuality is divorced from this incredible process. Being afraid makes the pain much worse and makes your stamina unknowable.

There was a traffic jam of births at the city hospitals the week I had my daughter. It was about nine months after the big earthquake hit San Francisco, and apparently staying home had been a fertile pastime during that otherwise sobering period. The other women who had children the day and night I was in the hospital did not appear to have husbands at their sides. It was easy for me to imagine their stories: they were single; they were lesbian; they had husbands who didn't want to see them that way; they had husbands who had left them earlier in their pregnancies; they had husbands in the service and far away.

I didn't read a single parenting book that reflected any of these lives, although they are as commonplace as conception itself. The fractured fairy tale ("Mommy and Daddy love each other very much") is only resonant in the sense that parents need to be loved and nurtured, because they are about to give of themselves in a way that they never dreamed possible before.

If the mother doesn't receive tenderness and passion during her nine months, the bitterness she develops lasts well beyond childbirth—her kids will know all about it. Perhaps I could encourage childbirth professionals to advocate good sex during pregnancy as a key to psychologically healthy children.

After the birth, you will get doctor's instructions to abstain from sex for the next six weeks. We've all heard the woman who says, "I don't care if I don't have sex for the next six years." But if her pussy is so sore, why can't she enjoy oral sex? Her breasts are leaking colostrum, ready to start expressing milk, and they need to be sucked by someone who knows about sucking breasts—babies don't always get the hang of it instantly, or at mom's command.

The truth is, this six weeks rule is arbitrary, and it's based on the fear of an infection resulting from a man ejaculating inside the vagina. There is a lot more to "sex" than this. Nothing magic happens at the end of six weeks. Not everyone's os and vaginal passageway are in the same condition after birth. Having had a Cesarean, mine had not been through a full-blown vaginal birth. Without knowing exactly what risk I was taking, but knowing that the doctor didn't know what he was talking about either, I came home from the hospital and made love on the sixth day after my daughter was born.

I've spoken with many women who admitted the same. "My husband and I had waited so long for this child," said my nurse practitioner/midwife, who had a child after she was forty, "that we had to be intimate right away." I appreciated her using the word "intimate," because I don't think it's the case that you just have this wild hare to get it on once the baby is born. You want a closeness, a release, and a celebration that you haven't necessarily experienced during labor.

My midwife also told me that she started asking her patients how soon after childbirth they had resumed intercourse. Lots of people break the rules, as you can imagine, and she found that women who had intercourse earlier on also resumed periods much sooner than those who waited. This little discovery—from a professional who wouldn't ordinarily tell me such things—reminded me again how little we know because no one shares taboo information.

Nursing is another source of mixed feelings, erotic and otherwise. One women winces in pain from chapped and bleeding nipples, while another has orgasms from her baby's suckling. Again, if these things were brought out in the open, a lot of nipple soreness would disappear. Breast

105

feeding does *not* come instinctively, and it helps to have someone show you as well as tell you how to nurse comfortably.

I was satisfied just to nurse my baby competently. My erotic feelings came not so much from my baby's sucking as from feeling my breasts express themselves at other times. Sexual arousal will make your breasts leak when you're lactating, another important fact missing in most parent handbooks. As much as I have lectured on G-spot orgasms, I had never had anything come *out* of me when I was making love before, and this made my head swim with embarrassment at first and then arousal.

I've always been one of those women who could be secretive about her climax. I could come without crying out. I could be very sneaky. Having my nipples not just stiffen, but release milk like a faucet every time I was turned on took me for a very un-private loop. But I loved rubbing it on my lover's chest, or my own. I felt some feminine equivalent of virility, making the biggest wet spot of them all. This was the very opposite of being hooked up to the electric breast pump, which made me feel like a working cow. Handy, but totally unerotic.

It would be unfair to conclude the erotic disposition of pregnancy without talking about changes in sexual fantasies. Our fantasies often seem to be written in stone at an early age and are not too easily transformed in our adult years. But having a baby is the next big hormone explosion a woman can have after puberty, and she may surprise herself with what comes to mind at the moment of orgasm. I did.

In retrospect I see that my fantasy life during my pregnancy was cathartic. One of my biggest and most irrational reservations about having a child (besides fearing that I would die in childbirth) was that if I had a boy, I wouldn't know how to raise him. I would be a disaster, whether teaching him how to use the toilet or to fly a kite.

Petty sexual stereotypes aside, I didn't know what little boys were like. I have no brothers, was raised by my mom, and always preferred dresses.

I'm a single parent, but I had conversations with the father of my kid now and then during my pregnancy. He was concerned that I was planning a politically correct dress code for the young one. "If it's a girl, I suppose you'll always make her wear pants," he pouted.

"Oh no," I said. "If I have a little girl, I'm going to make sure she has the frilliest, laciest, puffiest dresses you ever saw," remembering the kind of dresses I always wanted.

"And if it's a little boy," he started.

"Of course," I interrupted, "He'll have the frilliest, laciest, puffiest. . ."

My teasing was just a cover. I really didn't know what little boys were supposed to wear.

One night, I was making love with my friend, John, and I imagined that he was my son. I came like a rocket, and I didn't have the nerve to tell him about it for weeks. In the meantime, I could not get this image off my mind. I recalled a really tacky porn movie I had seen years ago, *Taboo*, where beautiful mom Kay Parker has a son (in real life, a grown-up actor named Mike Ranger) who only has eyes for her. I wasn't aroused by the movie the first time I saw it, but now this scene could turn me on instantly. I couldn't masturbate or make love to anyone, man or woman, without conjuring up this incestuous exchange.

At the same time, while making my plans for the baby and talking to friends and family, I was noticeably more at ease about having a boy child. I didn't know what sex my baby was, and unlike so many other moms, I didn't want to know.

I started noticing mothers with their sons on the street, and I didn't panic; I smiled at them. Somebody gave me a book on how to be a "dad," with all sorts of fabulous hints on butch activities from skipping stones to throwing a ball. I read the whole thing and thought it was a blast. I asked all my friends how many of them had fathers who did any of these things, and our answers shed a lot of light on our gender points of view.

When my team of doctors finally pulled Aretha from my womb, they were exuberant. "It's a girl!" somebody said. I was shaking very badly from the anesthesia, but this warm little yolk of feeling spilled in my head, and tears of relief came to my eyes. I was so pleased to have a daughter.

When I came home and had my first chance to fantasize (something sleep deprivation cut into quite a bit), I could not for the life of me conjure up my imaginary son! He had split. My incest fantasy had expressed my fear of having a boy, and when that possibility disappeared, the fantasy lost its magic. I don't know what would have happened to my fantasy if I had indeed come home with a son. I think I would have moved on, just as I did after Aretha's birth, to new sets of anxieties which became fresh erotic fodder.

Now I fantasize about being pregnant again—talk about kinky. In reality I have no desire to be eating soda crackers for a month and having to go to the bathroom every ten minutes for the next half year. But I do have glowing memories of the sexual discoveries I made during pregnancy, and I'm grateful I had a sexually loving and inquisitive support system around me. If the whole process could be like that. . . . Well, maybe I'll have another one, I tell myself, when my daughter is old enough to change the diapers.

WHEN NO MEANS
I DIDN'T KNOW IT WOULD
BE LIKE THIS

I don't get very many opportunities to speak in the South. When a graduate student named Karen invited me to speak to gay and lesbian students at her Southern university, I was very curious.

"How many people are in the Gay Student Union?" I asked.

"Well, I'm just about it," she said. "I mean, there's lots of folks who will come hear you, but most people here aren't out of the closet."

"Anybody besides you?" I asked again.

She thought for a moment. "No."

The leaflet for my talk was bright pink, but it didn't include the words "lesbian" or "gay." "If you put 'gay' on it," Karen explained, "then none of the gay people will come." I began to worry whether *anyone* would have a clue about the subject of my lecture.

"How will they know it's not a Chinese cooking demonstration?" I asked her.

She laughed at my apprehension. "Don't worry, the place will be packed."

And it was. Word of mouth brought out every possible lesbian within a hundred miles of campus, plus a whole contingent of Bohemian heterosexuals. I haven't spoken to such a warm, familial college group in ages. It's so different at Yankee schools. The typical outspoken Ivy League lesbo of the Northeast hates all the other queers on campus, except her girlfriend, and they are so bored with porno debates and fistfucking techniques that the most invigorating thing they've done all semester is open their mouths for a great big yawn.

A lesbian couple came up to me after my talk, both women with cheeks as pink as my compact and honey blond hair. "They're Episcopalian," Karen told me later, whatever that means. My mother always told me Episcopalians were upper-class Catholics. Here, I wasn't so sure. Most of this Southern audience, queer and liberal as it was, belonged to a church; it wasn't just these two.

Elise, the taller one, introduced me to her sweetheart. "Mary had a vision as you were speaking," she said. That didn't sound very Episcopalian. Mary's eyes were indeed shining, and her head bobbed up and down. I took a step back, bracing myself against a folding chair. I nodded at her like I heard this sort of thing all the time.

"It's her third one," Elise explained. "She saw the face of Jesus, once here at home and once at Lourdes, but this one was different."

Mary finally spoke for herself. "You were in the middle of your talk," she said, "and it was all so interesting—I don't remember which part it was—when I saw something bright shining over your right shoulder and, as I stared at it, I saw that it was a cross, a very ornate white cross that grew more and more luminous. I tried to stare further into it so I could figure out the nature of the design, but it grew too bright, and then it disappeared."

This woman was very articulate and her gaze was as steady as a rock.

"What did that make you think?" I asked her.

"At first, I thought that it meant that you were protected, and then it also occurred to me that it might mean you were a martyr."

I made a face at her last suggestion.

"But how does it make you feel?" she asked.

"I'm not sure," I said. "I really don't believe in visions,

but I like the idea of being protected, especially *here*. You must have been very moved by what I was saying to experience something like that, so it's a very big compliment, at the least. . . ." I trailed off. I had a lot of hard decisions to make when I got home from this trip. But if I had a white cross sitting on my right shoulder, maybe I would slay my dragons easily. I grabbed her vision like a good luck charm, like a psychic bulletproof vest.

After my talk, a few of us went off to the town's—no, make that the *state's*—only gay bar. It was a huge warehouse, with no windows or ventilation, surrounded by a big mud parking lot. Ford LTDs were the model of choice. "Takes me back," I yelled out the car window. I never thought I would get nostalgic about the old California gay bars with their queers, fag bashers and cops all together in the same mud parking lot, waiting to score.

The cutest boy at this watering hole was tending bar. "He's straight," moaned one of my companions, and I was struck by the scrapbook-perfect scenario this was turning out to be. "Of course he's straight," I said, "Y'all play by the book here."

The sexiest girls were boys, and they sat together in their gowns at one of a dozen long cafeteria-style tables. There was a small dance floor almost dwarfed by the disco ball glittering above it. The DJ alternated disco with country singles, and my toes were tapping. Yeah, maybe some fabulous butch would sweep in here and two-step me away into honey tongue land! My eyes wandered back to the bright red talons tip-tapping at the next table. If anything butch walked in here I'd lose out to the queens in two minutes.

I squinted a little harder through the smoke on the dance floor to see if I was counting right. Every male couple on the floor was waltzing and turning expertly with all the little flourishes, while the four women couples I could identify were either trying to hold onto each other without bumping into anyone or, in one case, carrying on a modern dance interpretation.

"These stereotypes have gone too far!" I yelled, pounding my fist on the picnic table. I got a splinter for my effort. I felt like I was trapped in one of those Wild Kingdom shows where the male of the species gets all the pretty feathers and fun while the peahens are completely idiotic. No one heard my yelling, but Karen saw the look on my face.

"If you want to talk, let's get out of here," she gestured, and we exited past the posters for Statewide Gala Empress Coronations.

Karen didn't have an LTD; she had a VW bug. She rolled down the window so we could feel the wet air on our faces. "Some of the women from campus wanted to know if you would be willing to ride on the bed for tomorrow's bed race," she said. "It's really a political thing—you'd carry a sign—no one is doing it to win."

"A bed race?" I asked. Was that like being the princess on the pea?

"It's an annual spring event," she said. "They close Main Street, and everyone races each other on rolling bed frames. All the fraternities and pizza parlors and such sponsor a bed, you see, and this year the Women's Center at the U. wanted to enter a special bed that would say something about date rape."

I imagined my own little iron poster number flying down the street in a blur. "What are they going to do, show a date rape in progress?" I knew I shouldn't be cavalier, but her explanation of the pageantry had me carried away.

She wasn't offended. "This is a long story, but you'd better hear it now, I guess," she said. "This is the biggest thing that's ever hit this campus.

"This university's pride and joy is the basketball team. . ." she began. I had a feeling I knew what was coming.

"That's why all the alumni give money," she went on,

"and that's why, when you asked me what this university was known for, I told you basketball."

"There are lots of schools like that," I said, thinking of my occasional reading of *Sports Illustrated*. The story Karen related was one I'd read many times before. Local team goes out to celebrate. Everyone gets blotto. Woman from town fools around with some of the boys. They take her back to the dorm—her free will—and sex is on the agenda. Sex with more than one player is also on the agenda. And yet this is where things start to unravel. The woman stops having a good time and starts having a real bad time. No one cares or pays any attention to her pain. No one really knows how many guys fucked her. *Tra La La*.

Next day it all gets reported, and now the story explodes. All the ballplayers are questioned by the administration and the police. Some are scared and confess to a gang bang; others keep their mouths shut. The honest are punished and suspended. They happen to be some of the best players on the team. The university, alumni and town are apoplectic—this "slut" is ruining their winning season. The few non-sport-centric citizens and parents are revolted by this sordid peek into campus social life. The hypocrisy stinks to high heaven.

Such campus disgraces repeat themselves over and over at every sort of college. In each case, great attention is paid to whether the woman is more virgin or whore. The attitudes of the administrations run a short spectrum from paternal to permissive. As the moral fabric goes on sale for ninety-nine cents a yard, often another voice is heard loud and clear, a voice that names the crisis as more than a scandal. This is the voice of the feminists, and they cry "date rape." They demand the integrity of a woman's right to say no to sex—at any point that she doesn't like what's going down. What's so refreshing about the feminist challenge is that it views the problem as one of consensuality, not promiscuity. But consent—or refusal—is not always as clear as a stop sign. Many date rape theorists have been loathe to discuss the complex dilemma of sexual negotiation or the shame women feel about acknowledging any desire or physical pleasure whatsoever. Women are always asked to choose between protection and risk, liberty and caution. Having little sexual confidence, most women don't have a chance given choices like these.

"So what would I do on this bed?" I asked.

"Mostly just hold up a sign," she said. "'When I Say No, It Means No!'— something like that."

"Well, when I say 'No,' it doesn't necessarily mean 'No'; sometimes it means—" I stopped. I looked at Karen to see if I could read her mind very quickly. How much did she know about sex and playing "pretend"? "I couldn't carry a sign like that," I continued. "It sounds like Nancy Reagan or Tipper Gore in her daughter's bedroom. Why can't I carry something that says, 'Why Can't Women Say Yes Without Duress?'"

"Well, it hardly matters anyway," Karen said, "because I don't think they're going to get their bed together in time. Besides, some of the Women's Center people don't think you are appropriate, being a pornographer and all."

"That's par for the course," I said, throwing caution to the wind. "Do you believe every 'No' you hear in bed?" I asked her.

"No," she smirked.

"It's hard for me to take 'No' at face value," I said. "This whole 'Feminism Means No' movement represents the puritanical side of the sex debates we've been having for ten years. As long as women don't have confidence about wanting sex, these 'No's' are always going to be very ambiguous. When I say 'No,' I have to ask, what is the context?"

"I think everyone at these frat parties knows exactly what the context is, and it's always the woman's word against the men's. Her word, her 'No,' is never as important." Karen wasn't quite so blasé about this after all.

I was quiet for a little bit. We were almost to my hotel parking lot. I felt defensive about being rejected by the local feminist powers-that-be, and Karen wasn't even breathing down my neck. Why do I always feel like I have to show them the blood left under my nails from when I said "No" to some man—some man bigger and stronger than me, who didn't pay me any mind? I took all those self-defense classes; I kicked the feminist stuntman with the padded suit right in the balls. Sometimes I was even creative, like the time I went to a nightclub with razors pinned to my breast. Leave me the fuck alone.

Karen didn't seem to be in a big hurry. We sat in the dark of the hotel lot and she lit a cigarette.

"I've always been afraid of the bullies," I told her. "Nothing really made a dent in my fear, not all the kicking, screaming and whistles. What changed me was visiting my first strip show. I was scared, of course, even to go in. I was afraid of the men inside. I went with another dyke who had no such qualms. We were the only women in the theater with our clothes on. The women on stage and in the aisles were shaking, shimmying and sticking it all out, and I could see the men in the edge of their spotlight watching them in total awe. Their bluntness, their ability to be sexually aggressive and maintain limits at the same time, was the complete opposite of the sexual intimidation of the date rape scenario." I wondered if Karen believed me.

"Men can still be brutes, you know—taking physical advantage of sorority girls and burlesque queens." Karen nodded impatiently.

"Look," I said. "I'm trying to tell you that I can't stop the basketball team from going ape shit, but I'll be damned if they—or anyone else—will destroy my sexual spirit. I am *not* going back to the fifties."

I had to shut up before the white cross on my shoulder fell over and cracked. Maybe I could *show* Karen what I meant.

"Is there a strip tease joint in this town?" I asked.

"No way!" Karen laughed, and reached for my hands. "You turn me on," she said. "Can you tell?"

So that's why I felt so nervous. She didn't care about my political diatribe.

"What about how in love you are with your new girlfriend?" I asked. Her new lover was her first femme, sex was the best ever, true love, etc. . . .

"I know, but I talked to her about you," Karen said. "About how if we weren't monogamous. . . ."

"Oh, please, I don't even want to hear this—that means you were talking about me before I even got here!" I hate it when couples use you as fodder for their make-believe peccadilloes and then tell you about it—as if you could actually play an equal third in the fantasy.

She brushed my nipples easily. There were no bucket seats between us. "We could kiss," she said.

"No means 'No'!" I made a face at her. But I did not move away. I felt bored, aggravated, curious, and pressured all at the same time. "You'll just go tell her, and then she'll be upset, and when I see you again in our extremely small world, I will feel like I've violated your perfect little relationship." A vomit-green diatribe against couples was rising up.

"I won't tell her," she said.

"No?"

"Not if you care so much."

"Liar, liar, pants on fire."

When I was seventeen, I thought good sex was worth whatever you had to go through later. A year later I changed my mind. Now I was thirty-three and my white cross was wavering. Her fingers on my breast made me feel defiant, reckless. I lifted my head towards hers. No Means Kiss Me.

She did.

"I'm wet now," I said, pulling away from her, "and I don't care about your perfect girlfriend." Karen ran her hand under my legs. I wasn't lying. I sighed.

She stopped kissing me.

"I can't," she said.

"What do you mean, you *can't?* Are you kidding?"

She wasn't. My stomach cramped.

"I'm sorry," she said. "I can't do this to Mary."

The shame of the predictable overwhelmed me. I wanted to say, "We're not in that silly bar anymore; we don't have to read our lines."

But instead I got out of the car and asked her when she would pick me up to go to the airport the next morning.

That night in my room I saw the REM video, "Losing my Religion," on MTV. I remembered I'd overheard somebody use that expression that morning in the breakfast place where Karen had taken me. It's Southern for going too far, getting out of hand. "Connie lost her religion over that one," they'd said, and I had smiled and wondered whether it was an extramarital affair or a closet case on the rocks.

But maybe Connie had just lost her false sense of security, like me or like a woman who walked into a bar and flirted with the wrong bunch of guys. That white cross could make you into a martyr, no problem, or even just a fool. It offered me no protection, but it sure was an impressive reminder of the risks.

The next day Karen couldn't stop apologizing and I couldn't stand it.

"Hey, I didn't know it was going to be like this," I said. Make a sign that says *that* and I'll carry it anywhere. "I'll see you and your girl in San Francisco," I promised, though I never would. I picked up my bags and my cross, and flew back home.

LYNNIE IS THE QUEEREST THING ON THIS STREET

Bernal Heights is a pretty quiet neighborhood these days. A few months ago, someone bought the Beatle house, a stucco two-story down the street that sported a spectacular roof-to-cellar mural of the Beatles legend, from Hamburg to "Let It Be." The new owners have painted it gray. A block down from the Beatle house is Patty Hearst's SLA hideout, and across from that house is the formerly-notorious "Needle Park." The hot topic at Precita Park today is whether or not to build a low fence around the children's playground. I still stumble over a beer can in the sandbox now and then, but it's just not the same. It really hasn't been the same since Lynn left. It's been a decade since I met Lynn, and eight years since she moved away.

Gay Day morning, 1981. I had a packed house, with dykes from Santa Cruz sleeping in the living room. I always feel so civic-minded and hospitable on Gay Day. Strawberry pancakes must be made for everyone. Parade participants must have their buttons pinned on clean and tight. Triumphant music must be played on the stereo, and every sentimental tradition of the past decade of Gay Days must be observed. Most importantly, it's my roommates' anniversary. On this day two years ago, they stuck a wad of opium up their butts and fell madly in love. Now one goes to AA and the other to Al-Anon, but their story must be lovingly repeated.

At seven I sneaked into the living room like Santa on

that Gay Day morning to see if any of my friends' heads were peeking out of their sleeping bags yet. Wait 'till they smelled the pancakes. It was during these few minutes of quiet, just before the whole city came alive for the biggest parade of the year, that I was at my most excited. I went back to the kitchen to get the strawberries and considered whether I should put the first one in my mouth or my pussy.

Something smashed into a million pieces outside. I heard a whole lot of breaking glass, and a voice just as sharp right after it.

"Drop the knife, motherfucker!"

I didn't understand those words at first. I only pieced them together later by asking my five formerly-prone sleeping bag guests who now had their faces pressed against our front door and windows. It was a girl's voice, young but low, and it sounded like she had a mouthful of golf balls. She also sounded like she meant business.

In the middle of the street was Neil, and that was bad news. Neil was some sort of Agent Orange disaster area. He lived in the park, he was always fucked up, and he tried to get little girls to take down their drawers for him. You didn't sit down with him and have a big old talk about the war, because he was almost rabid. Sure enough, he was waving a butcher knife and snot was running down his chin. He was half-crying, half-yowling like a pissed cat. Something about "Jewish bitches." His paranoia had an aura the color of his mucus.

Standing not two yards away from him, facing uphill on Manchester Street, was a wiry little blonde shag number with blood dripping off one of her clenched fists. I looked up at the house behind her and at the glass shards; she had apparently punched out the front door. This was our neighbor!

She was talking to Neil again, her voice still demanding, but even and steady now, as if breaking the window had calmed her.

"How come I don't understand a word she's saying?" I asked.

"She's from Brooklyn," one of my roommates said.

"What part of Brooklyn is that?" someone else asked, and I wanted to know the same.

Neil still held his knife in his outstretched hand, his voice coming in gasps and full of high-pitched exclamations.

"That's it, man," the blonde said. She walked straight into that snot-green zone that separated the two of them and grabbed Neil's knife out of his hand like he was a baby. He let her! Then she cursed and cuffed him, and by the time I finished saying, "I can't believe my eyes," they had disappeared through the broken door.

Years later, I asked Lynnie, "Did you know it was Gay Day that morning you took Neil's knife away?"

"Shit no, I didn't know Gay nothing 'till I met you *dykes* across the street," she said. "I'll never forget that, you saying that *word* to me."

I can't forget it either. I'd stared at the blue house across the street a million times, but the shades were always closed, and it didn't look like that front door was ever going to have more than a piece of plywood tacked over it. It was one of the Victorians that gentrification had spared. One day after work, I was trudging up from the corner store and that mobster drawl came floating down over my head like a butterfly.

"Hey, dollface, how ya doin'?"

Dollface? Not only could she pull that off, but she gave me goosebumps, too. She was leaning out the window of the second story and grinning. I could see her face up close now, the face of a comic book superhero. Strong jaw, deep-set green eyes that *twinkled*, for Christ's sake, button nose, and that blond rocker shag I'd noticed before. Her sweatshirt had the arms cut out and she had superhero biceps too. I was Lois Lane Dollface and I was falling fast.

"Can I come up?" I asked.

"Yeah, just a minute," she said, and disappeared. I waited longer than it could possibly take for her to walk downstairs and open the door. That broken door was staring at me like one of those dream doors you're not sure you want to walk through. When Lynn finally opened it, she was wearing a happy coat kimono, the short kind, only this one was pulled down to one side by a .45 automatic stuck in her silk pocket. You know, with Lynn there was never time to get shocked. You were immediately put into accelerated nonchalance because she was moving so fast.

"What's that for?" I asked, nodding to the gun, and then climbing the stairs, "What's your name?"

"Lynn," she said, and as if on cue, some little girl bawled, "LYN-NIE!"

"That's Leah," she explained. "I take care of her while her ma's at work."

Leah stuck her head around the corner to check me out. Maybe eight years old, with her hands covered in make-up. Lynn said something to her about whining, and Leah walked off pouting. I'll never be able to report half the things Lynn said around me, because I couldn't translate her speech very well.

The gun had to do with the pot, she told me, waving her arms towards the back yard where, sure enough, there stood a greenhouse and several plants six feet high. They were being vandalized, she said, all these fuckers who she'd been so generous to were trying to mess with her, and this was going to put a halt to it—the gun, that is.

Lynn was talking about the same stupid prepubescent boys who messed with all the neighbors' cars, flower boxes and pot plants. She seemed to be acquainted with the juvenile delinquents a little better than most of us. This apartment was obviously the neighborhood crash pad. In fact, I got the idea that Neil was probably Lynn's only grown-up visitor so far. Lynn looked like a high school kid herself, but she told me she was twenty-five.

She took me to the bedroom that faced the street. There was a foam mattress on the floor, oils and incense and purple velvet books, and a Stevie Nicks cassette. "This is Linda's room," Lynn explained, although she didn't have to. It was too feminine for her.

Seeing the traces of the woman in her life cooled me off. I didn't think I could ask her to call me "dollface" again and fuck my brains out on a handmade comforter that smelled like a Linda.

Lynn went to get an album cover to roll a joint, and never stopped talking about the trials and tribulations of her pot-growing scheme. Leah came in to stare at me some more, and I told her I had a big Christmas case of Princess Borghese make-up that she could have. Instant kinship.

Lynnie handed me an enormous joint and I asked her why she hung out with Neil. There was no understanding a word that came out of her mouth, but her tone was that of an exasperated but forgiving daddy. Neil was like a little girl to her. She was by nature the butchest thing I'd ever seen and her unconsciousness of her masculinity only made her more so. She wasn't going to be able to call herself a tomboy for too many more years, I thought. What would happen then?

She passed me a little onyx pipe. "What's this?" I said, not recognizing the smell. "Hash," she said, and the next thing I found out about Lynn was that she was a pathological liar.

The hit I took went through me like an ice blast and I thought my bowels were going to fall out on the floor. I guess it felt worse than it really was, because I ran without tripping all the way to the bathroom. What should have been a chemically euphoric moment was scaring the shit out of me. I felt like the kid in those drug movies who got in way over his head.

"What the fuck was that?" I asked her when I finally

emerged from the can. She ignored me.

Linda was home. She was a bigger version of Leah, all big brown eyes and fluffy dark hair, some of it graying.

I ran to the window to see if my home was still across the street. I saw Jackie climbing up the hill with her groceries. Jackie lived two doors up, and she was the first person I met the day I moved onto Manchester Street. "Hi, I'm Jackie," she said, "and I'm on my way to an SOL meeting."

"What's SOL?" I asked.

"Slightly Older Lesbians," she said, and winked. "You can't come yet." She was over sixty.

I laughed remembering my introduction to the neighborhood and decided to try to find some common ground again with Miss .45.

"Isn't it incredible how many dykes live on this street?" I said.

"WHAT!—WHAT did you say!" Lynn yelled with the biggest golf ball ever in her larynx. "LIN-DAAAAAA!" She ran into the next room, bellowing "Linda" like it was "STELL-LA!" Marlon Brando wouldn't have a chance next to these lungs. She dragged Linda to the scene of the crime, like I'd shit on the carpet.

"You're not going to believe what she just said, the word she says to me, I can't believe it." Clearly Lynn couldn't even repeat it, my terrible word.

I felt like checking the calendar. This *was* 1983 in San Francisco and I could walk into any Irish bar in the Mission and say "dyke" without a soul looking up. I had made a big mistake here, though.

"I'm sorry I said that," I offered. "I was stupid, I assumed you two were together and that you must know the other lesbians"—I enunciated 'lesbians' very neatly— "who live on this street. I'm very, very sorry I offended you."

Linda picked up a roach from the bookshelf and lit it,

without looking at me. I figured it was bye-bye time. Lynn grabbed my arm as I bent to pick up my sweater. "No, no, I'm going to walk you home," she said, as if I lived across the railroad tracks.

I was about to protest, but this was the first time she had touched me. That was all I needed to remember why I was in this crack den to begin with. Under my skin, that's where Lynn lived.

She held my hand as she walked me to my door and whispered, like I was her special confidante, "I'm sorry about Linda being so cold, you know, we've been fighting and shit. . ."

"What are you talking about?" I said, not whispering. "You ARE a couple? Or what? *Why?*" I was sputtering. "If you two are together, then what was I apologizing for, calling you a fucking dyke! You're the queerest thing on this street!"

"Well, we don't call it nothing," she said, not quite so self-righteous this time. "I never met anybody who called themselves that."

And that was the truth, probably the first time I'd heard the truth that afternoon. I told her to come over to my house later; I had Princess Borghese and a few other dykes I'd like to introduce her to.

LYNNIE AND THE
KAMIKAZE HEART

There were a lot of stories about Lynnie. The biggest whopper was that she was going to die any day now. There certainly was an ugly bump sticking out of her scalp. She said it was a brain tumor. Sometimes it swelled up and caused her terrible pain. But she hasn't died yet. The doctors at Stanford were treating her experimentally, someone said, which afforded her a liberal prescription for pharmaceutical cocaine. They'd told her several times she was going to die in six months, so what was the point in telling her to cool it with the coke?

I heard she had been on her own since she was fourteen, and that she had endeared herself to this older guy who died and left her a lot of money, and that's why she had all the drugs in the world. I couldn't imagine her being any guy's child-mistress, so if it was anything sexual, he must have been worshiping the untouchable.

One thing I knew for sure was that her father was a milkman in Brooklyn. He came out to see her once with her little brother, and they seemed awfully boring compared to her. Her mom was dead.

My household invited Linda and Lynn to their first lesbian party. Then we took them to their first lesbian bar, and finally, Lynnie got in tight with the druggie dyke strippers downtown and procured a job as a bouncer at one of the sleaziest needle-chasing peep shows on Market Street. If you changed a light bulb there, you'd find someone's works. This was 1984, before Raven and Beth and Pam died in one horrible year and everybody else joined Narcotics Anonymous. The good-old bad-old days.

Obviously, Lynn could stir up as much trouble at this job as she could prevent. But her disarming quality with Neil, the neighborhood psycho, was evident in all her dealings with the men who came to the Market Street Cinema. She brought out the boy in them; they responded not to Mommy, but to Daddy. After she slapped the naughty ones around a little, they wanted to impress her.

Lynn was the total opposite of the political, communal lesbians I grew up with. I felt like some finishing school Bluebell by comparison. I couldn't help but see in her the kind of bottom-line dyke that has been all but milque-toasted out of existence in yuppie lesbian life. Her camaraderie with men—studs or queens—was a refreshing contrast to the lace curtain separatism that the mainstream lesbian community endorsed.

She did not approach all women equally. She was only attracted to femmes; they brought out the hero in her. Her romanticism and the protectiveness she showed her girlfriends was brazen, completely unfeminine.

She had her combative social relationships with other butches, whom she called "dykes." I hated her competitiveness with the few other women who resembled her. I figured they ought to be best friends, the last of a breed— but she would have none of it. Her only way of making friends with another butch was to pick a fight and then make up over bruised heads. I didn't like it, but it was queer as a pulp novel.

There is an independently produced movie, *Kamikaze Hearts*, that plays at big city repertory theaters every so often. It was shot on location at the Market Street Cinema, and it has footage of Lynn losing her temper and mixing it up with another "chick," as she would say.

Kamikaze is a semi-documentary about two lesbian lovers/porn stars and their tumultuous time on the set of a rinky-dink porn movie. The movie was controversial when it came out, because it shows mega drug use in connection with making porn. I'm sorry if everyone is so shocked and dismayed, but if similar movies were made about drug use in Hollywood, on MTV, or in professional football, perhaps the point would hit home: It's not porn that is so drug-crazed, it's the entertainment business.

Tigr and Mitch are the star-crossed, coke-bleary lovers of *Kamikaze Hearts*. At one point Mitch, about to shoot up, holds up her needle to the camera. Explaining her relationship with Tigr, she says: "This is my dick. She wanted my dick and I gave it to her."

I saw this film once with an all-lesbian audience, who booed like a bunch of old ladies at the tewwible, tewwible drug abuse this movie portrays. But Mitch's lines made me cry—though not about drugs. My sadness was about Mitch's real dyke dick and about being a butch and about how you have to give your girl what she wants.

Lynn's big moment in the movie shows her in a fist fight with another girl in the aisles as the strip show plays on. The adrenalin breaks across her brow in a shine, and you can tell she *has* to hit something. A few quick cuts later, we see her flushed and elated outside the theater doors, and you don't know whether she's been victorious or taken her lumps. Lynn has to have the impact, one way or the other, or there's no relief for her.

What is it about violence and women who don't shy away from it? When I get mad, I'm such a *girl*; it all turns inward. Bitchy sarcasm is the only bite I've got. The rest worms inside of me, doubting and cramping and trying to understand.

Of course, my feminine position is superior to violent behavior: violence is no way to settle an argument. I'm not a caveman; I can talk about my feelings. But sometimes I envy the short, quick, decisive burst: the fury that seems to say it all so quickly.

I never like to be around when anyone loses their temper; in the aftermath, something comes undone in me as well.

One time a man I loved provoked a street fight as we were walking home after the bars closed. He came to me afterwards with such a bloody face, saying, "Lick it off, baby." And I did, like a mother cat. Lynn tried to pull me in like that a million times, and I always resisted—I could not mother her.

Lynn and Linda eventually ran up so many credit card scams in San Francisco that one week they packed up very quickly and moved to Arizona. I heard they were using heroin, too. Little Leah, Linda's daughter, was getting bounced around to different parts of the family, going crazy, and that made me sick. They were both blaming each other.

I had quite sobered up from my idea that if Lynnie came out of the closet she would somehow clean up her act. First, she was a Class A addict. Second, she never, never joined the life of the gay middle class.

My friend Allan told me once that gay society was his introduction to the finer aspects of the middle class: education, art, fine cooking, the works. He, like many others, was grateful. Lynn was never attracted to any of that, though; she was a poet who didn't care for aesthetics. She wanted her piece of land with no one else on it. Her cowboy ideals made her feel "straight." She never called herself "gay," and she never made it with a man.

Lynn wrote me rhyming verses from Arizona and sent photos of the houses she was building, of land she was buying. She said she had split up with Linda and was happy for it. But she sounded awfully lonely. She finally came out again to San Francisco for more of her experimental brain tumor tests. I guess they paid her way because her case was so unusual.

I told Lynnie that I was moving into a new apartment that had to be completely repainted, and she said she could do the whole thing for me in a couple of hours. There was no way to stop Lynn from "helping" you once she set her mind to it. Helpfulness is another classic butch quality and goes a step beyond having a man around the house. A butch *has* to help out, and god help you if she isn't competent. If she helps you, then she loves you, and you have to accept this love unconditionally. A man in this situation behaves similarly, though he is usually a little more uptight about his expertise and not nearly so joyful about the result.

Lynn was at my flat singing and painting for six hours. She covered not only the walls but also the entire floor with paint. My roommate Jill, another butch, came home and they hated each other instantly. By this time, it only made me jolly. If they would punch each other in the nose a couple of times I was sure they'd be the best of friends.

Now that the apartment was soaking wet in flat white latex, Lynn insisted we jam into her jeep and go to pick up her latest girlfriend, who happened to be attending high school on the other side of town. "That's new for you, Lynnie," I said. She usually only went for Mommas. Apparently this girl said she would take off with Lynn that night to drive back to Arizona. But her mother had to agree first. "I had an affair with her mother a long time ago," Lynn said. That explained everything.

I hadn't been on a high school campus for a long time. Lynnie had no qualms about going to the attendance office and demanding to know where this girl was. Spanish class, third floor, James Hall.

When we got to the classroom, though, Lynn was too afraid to go inside. "Just go in quietly and say you need a word with this young woman," I advised her. A minute later, a hippie girl with strawberry hair down to her waist appeared at the door, her face all lit up with excitement. Lynn was telling her a thousand details about getting out of town. "Give her my phone number," I said, "so she can reach you this afternoon."

"Oh, yeah, good idea," said Lynn, who proceeded to

carve my phone number into the classroom door.

"Jesus, Lynn," I hissed, "why don't you just add 'for a good time, call' so I can hear from every blow job acne-case in this entire school!"

But our mission was accomplished. Time to go back and check on the paint job. Lynnie asked me in the car if I'd always liked her. "You know I have," I said, "I just always liked Linda, that's all."

She started on the rag again about Linda's millions of faults, and I felt like the point was slipping away. Maybe I'd have to shock her again, like the first time we met. "Do you want to make love, when we get to my house?"

"Now?!" She turned beet red, which was funny because Lynn was always doing things *now*—it was planning ahead that wasn't her strong suit.

"Yeah, this afternoon, right now. There's nothing in my room but the bed, and Jill won't be home for a few hours."

I want to remember every detail of that afternoon with Lynn and I can't. The sun was shining right on the bed, where she lay like a lion. She was very proud of her body, of how strong she was. She could pick me up like a baby, and I was much taller than she was.

"What did you do to your eyebrows?" I asked, tracing these funny little crescents, almost all stubble.

"I shave them," she said. "You know, I have bushy eyebrows; I don't like the way it looks. I can't be bothered plucking them." It seemed she only liked the hair on her head, because she shaved the fine hair on her arms and legs too, like a swimmer.

On one side of her chest, between her collarbone and her shoulder, was a real ugly scar. "What's this from?" I asked. I didn't even touch it because it looked so sore.

She started one story, then another, and then she put my pillow over her head. I think the next part was the truth.

"My gun. . ." she said, "went off. . . well, I held it to

my mouth, but I'd been drinking, you know, and I must have fucked up."

The impact of that changed everything. One way or the other.

I had to gather her up like a child. I wanted to cuff her, and yell at her, like she had with Neil. But she hadn't had anyone to take that gun away from her, and she didn't stand on any mountain top and call out the names of her enemies.

I wanted to lick her life clean. I couldn't. One moment, I gazed at her almost like a savior, but then I eliminated that possibility forever. I could not hand out grace, and it was a comfort to know that ahead of time for a change.

I rocked her, kissing her, instead. "I don't come," she said. "Well, I did with Linda, but that was different."

"I knew you would say that," I said. "Just let me play with you a little, just for the hell of it."

The sun beating down made her pliant, perhaps. She let me. She squirmed and made a face when I rubbed between her lips. But she let me.

"I guess you don't masturbate, either," I said. Her eyes flew up in that same horror mask she made the first time I said the unspeakable word "dyke."

I could laugh now. "You and your gun, me and my vibrator!" I got out my magic wand, which I had installed as soon as the bed was up. She kept protesting, but she didn't stop me. I think she'd decided, for this one afternoon, that all rules were for breaking.

Her skin was fair, like mine, and broke out pink when she was aroused. I felt like her sister then. "You take this back with you to Arizona," I said, watching her tremble against all the buzzing in my hand. I could kiss her and kiss her and she didn't move away from me, or try to get on top. I didn't come either.

She left that night with Nancy, the high school girl, inviting me along, but no chance. I got a lot more letters from her after that, asking me to come to New Mexico. When I got pregnant a few months later, she insisted on it. We had a big fight, because for the first time I refused her help, and nothing could be more insulting.

She called me up smashed one night. I was big as a house and not the least bit compromising.

"Why don't you ever call me?" she yelled. "You're a fucking bitch!" Then she said "fucking bitch" about a thousand more times, and I hung up. Fucking Irish Catholic bitch. I was having a real baby o' my own very soon; no other babies allowed.

I love Lynnie. I don't know if it was cowardly to tell her I loved her and then hang up on her. I hung up on my own mother when I was pregnant—she was calling out names, too. Sticks and stones will break my bones but obscenities will always hurt me.

It's not the destruction and the damage that makes Lynn so dear to me; it's the life in her. It's that loudmouth bright yellow head, her tenaciousness—such a little girl/Daddy.

She told me so many whoppers. She called me Dollface, and she sang like a canary for six hours painting my flat. Her occasional and overriding truths were some of the most brutal I ever heard. I hope I'll have another word with Lynn someday. I want it to be the kind of word that makes her stand straight up, no eyebrows, yelling, "You fucking bitch! I'm free at last." And grace willing, I'll know that it's true.

LESBIANS, LIES, SECRETS AND SILENCE
(Or What Goes Around Comes Around)

It is a characteristic of the human mind that it tries to dichotomize in its classification of phenomena. Things either are so, or they are not so. Sexual behavior is either normal or abnormal, socially acceptable or unacceptable, heterosexual or homosexual; and many persons do not want to believe that there are graduations in these matters from one to the other extreme.

—Kinsey, 1953

Mention lesbians and AIDS. Unless you are talking to the leatherette avant-garde or the media watchdogs, you may get a smirk. Or perhaps a discussion will ensue about men's problems and men's sex. It's a traditional sentiment, that men are over-obsessed with sex. Therefore women, especially lesbians, fill in nicely as the ones who who have kept sex private, preserved its sensuality, and celebrated romantic purity. Cleanliness is next to Sappho-ness. Lesbians, according to conventional wisdom, don't get AIDS.

But don't be deceived. AIDS evokes strong emotions in lesbian consciousness: the unspoken fear of male contamination, a suspicion of contact with men, and the denial that follows from such fears. Scratch a little deeper, and you'll find loathing, contempt and hostility for masculinity

133

in general. If some of this hostility is well earned, some is a symptom of closet-case paranoia.

It's simply not true that lesbians aren't personally affected and infected by the AIDS virus. In 1990, when I traveled to Canada as a lesbian sex educator, my first stop was Ottawa. I didn't know much about the city except that the women's bookstore had only recently reversed its decision to carry lesbian erotica. There was no explicit information available for lesbians about AIDS.

The faces I saw that night at the local community center were so squeaky clean and wide-eyed that even *I* wondered if I were corrupting the innocent with my dental dam demonstration. After my lecture, I sat on a stool to autograph books and speak to people individually. The first woman in line wanted to talk about her four-year-old daughter's sexual curiosity. The second advice-seeker was having the damnedest time finding her G-spot. And the third woman, older than the rest, in a conservative blouse and skirt, bit her lip before she spoke to me. Her voice was just a whisper. "My lover left this morning," she said. She started to cry. I bent my head closer to hers so that our long hair made a little tent apart from the others. "I don't understand," I said, "what's the matter?"

"I got my diagnosis last Wednesday," she said. "I am. . . HIV-positive. . . Oh god, I don't know what to do. . . ." I didn't know what to do either. At that moment, I was as frightened as she was. She started to apologize. "Several years ago," she began, "I was out of work, and I shouldn't have done it, but—"

I put my fingers on her lips.

"Please don't tell me why you think you got infected. I don't care. You didn't do anything wrong."

She started crying in earnest. I was the only one she had confided to besides her lover, who had gone into shock for a week and had finally packed up her stuff the night before. No one knew about this woman's "past," and she felt she couldn't tell anyone now because she would lose her friends, all of them lesbian. She taught children in a daycare center—she was sure the center would not let her continue to work there if they knew. She had mentally canvassed her whole world and rehearsed the rejections she was sure she would get.

I felt a little crazy to be the first one to talk to her. I could hardly tell her to stop exaggerating and buck up, since I thought her fears were precisely in line with what she could expect. All I could tell her was that she would find exceptions.

"You will tell others," I told her. "I know you will, because it's the only way you're going to get through this. Your best friends are going to be the people who stand by you now. You're going to find new family, people who are going through the same thing you are. Most of them won't be lesbians, but they'll be closer to you than anyone."

I held her very tight. "No one can kick you out of this community," I said. "I'm sure you've been a lesbian longer than anyone else here!"

That made her laugh, which was good because my angry indignation act was not going to last very long. I didn't want to cry in front of her.

Finally, I let her go. A young blond co-ed walked up next for my autograph. "My new girlfriend says she can't be with me if I call myself bisexual." It was all I could do to keep from throwing her book against the wall.

Lesbians closely guard their sexual secrets to the point of estrangement from each other. These secrets are hidden behind a rather shaky public front of pre-AIDS feminist rhetoric, a rhetoric which hardly matches reality. Like most uneasy silences, this one is a killer, isolating one lesbian from the next. But the dam has burst. What one woman whispered to me in a Canadian prairie town two years ago is something I can hear any day of the week now: "I am losing girlfriends to AIDS."

How does such a supposedly tight-knit community keep such a secret among its own members? Perhaps by separating itself into imaginary camps: "real lesbians" (who have no contact with men or IV drugs) and "fallen angels." The Real Lesbian, much like the Emperor Who Wore No Undies, is little more than a political myth. Real Lesbians don't sleep with men or use needle drugs. Unthinkable. A lesbian who admits to either could get her dyke I.D. revoked faster than Chuck Connors got stripped in *The Rifleman*. If the straight world's prejudice is that AIDS is a "gay" disease, lesbians are even more xenophobic: AIDS belongs to men, not to us.

Statistically, only four cases of female-to-female sexual transmission of the virus have been recorded, and then only in medical journals. My friend in Canada will not be listed as a "lesbian" case, because it's unlikely she got infected through "lesbian" sex. Lesbians at risk? The popular opinion is that the average dyke would more likely fall off a truck.

Let's follow that truck. In 1987, women researchers at the Kinsey Institute made an unusual pilgrimage deep into the heart of lesbian America to find out what relationship lesbians really had to high-risk sex. They took their RV to a Midwestern women's music festival, otherwise known as "dyke summer camp." Every year, more than five thousand women attend the festival, and this year, several hundred women filled out detailed questionnaires about their sexual practices. The researchers discarded all surveys from women who said they were straight or bi. They only wanted to look at surveys from women who said they were lesbians. That left two hundred and sixty-two responses. These lesbians revealed several important secrets. Forty-six percent had had sex with men since 1980. What kind of heterosexual sex had they experienced? Fully one-third reported that their male partners were bisexual or gay. Over seventy percent had unprotected intercourse to

136

ejaculation with their male partners. Of all the lesbians who engaged in anal intercourse with men, only three consistently used condoms.

Twenty-eight percent of the women in the Kinsey study had called themselves lesbian from the time they were teenagers; nearly half of these women had had sex with men since age eighteen, twenty-one percent since 1980, when the American AIDS crisis began in earnest. The researchers noted in their report, "Lesbian women engage in high risk sexual behaviors less frequently than their heterosexual counterparts because they are less likely to have sex with men. However, at least for the women in this sample, when lesbians did interact sexually with men, they were likely to do so with high risk partners." Not to mention engaging in high risk sexual practices.

In other words, many people fall off the truck.

A lot of dykes point to the scarcity of female-to-female transmission and say "What, me worry?" The number-one lesson of this ever-expanding plague—it doesn't fucking matter how you got it—is as lost on the average dyke as it is on Jesse Helms. A lesbian who becomes sero-positive from risky contact with men or drugs confronts this disease *now*, in the context of her lesbian relationships and community. She's not about to check into a motel full of boys and syringes to live out the rest of her life.

Lesbians carry the burden of traditional feminine purity twice over. Like all women, we've been raised to preserve the values of innocence, chastity, and sexual propriety. We have been taught to be protective of our bodies and suspicious of sexual license. But as lesbians, our dose of sexual conservatism is squared. Our sexual preference is often equated with an irreversible disgust for male sexuality, its pornographic manifestations, and its disease-implicit consequences. The stereotype is that women must be lesbian because they couldn't stand it anymore: pricks, porn, the whole panoramic putz.

Let's look at the other high-risk lesbian group. While lesbians fucking men is the touchiest issue, needle drug use is also tainted with the stain of male vice. It's curious that even though lesbians are at a fever pitch of membership in twelve-step programs like Alcoholics Anonymous and Narcotics Anonymous, no one's asking, gee, if so many of us are attracted to getting high, why aren't lesbians shooting up? Do we think the dykes leave the party first? No way. Lesbians have such a spotless reputation that we are not usually associated with the harder vices. The double whammy of "feminine" conservatism is at work again. If the myth is that nice girls don't shoot up, then lesbians are ultra-nice.

Let's remember the sixties for a moment. Remember how drugs were supposed to relax our sexual inhibitions? Remember the haven gays found in unisex hippie culture? Now fast-forward to the seventies and eighties. Weren't drugs associated with some of the most androgynous and gender-bending stars of rock 'n' roll and of pop culture? Lesbians were there, and same-sex relationships were as common then as they are now. We didn't get sent off to some four-square finishing school for wholesome living. *We* helped make the counterculture, and drugs have always been part of it.

There has always been that impulse in the gay revolution—to throw out the rules and smash all the closets. But, ironically, the rules of gay life often turn out to be just as strict as those in any heterosexual courtship. Gay culture has carved out the territory it holds today by drawing boundaries. If you sleep with the opposite sex (or shoot dope), you're supposed to keep your mouth shut about it.

Why does a lesbian take a chance with HIV-infection? A lesbian fucks a man because it's a challenge, a curiosity, an attraction, a threat, an empathy. Yes, we could clinically call these women bisexual; we could line them up on the Kinsey scale, all those two's, three's, four's and five's deviating from the twin poles of heterosexuality and homosexuality. But in real life, people don't identify erotically with their sexual history print-out. They call themselves queer because of a particularly modern mixture of their sexual, affectional, cultural and political preferences. Real lesbians, like real people, are individuals. AIDS forces lesbians to admit that even occasional sexual contact with men (and even occasional needle use) leaves them outside the safety net of dyke purity. Lesbians have two practical choices: to be honest about lesbian-to-male contact and accordingly take protective measures, or to deny the truthful range of lesbian sexual activity. Of course, the virus doesn't give a fuck who you think you are: It's a disease. If the heartbreaking stereotype among straights is that AIDS is a "gay" disease, the corollary among lesbians is that lesbians who get AIDS are traitors; they were weak; they didn't keep the faith. The concept of male contamination requires lesbians to believe that they are *susceptible* to a more powerful sexual force.

I don't believe any of that, but I'm kept aware of those prejudices constantly. I think lesbians are lesbians because they have a desire for women that is only satisfied in an intimate union having nothing to do with being strong or weak, loyal or faithless. That union is supported by the lesbian community but lesbian desire, not the community, is the bottom line. Lesbian desire doesn't go away because you have sex with men. It doesn't go away because of a positive diagnosis. It never goes away.

I GOT THIS WAY
FROM KISSING DONAHUE

I first met Phillip at a baby shower. Our host led me over to a group of friends underneath a patio umbrella and pointed him out—the handsomest of the bunch. "You two have to meet because you have something very unusual in common," David explained.

"He's a pregnant lesbian sex expert?" I asked. I was eight months along and pretty cranky.

"Sort of," David whispered. "Phillip is gay, and he's having his first affair with a woman."

Phillip embraced me like a comrade. We looked into each other's eyes and he said, "I gather your baby's father is not just a sperm purveyor to you."

"Well, I'm not speaking to him right now," I said, "which, as you know, means I was very fond of him in the past."

Phillip was still in the stage where he was both fond of his girlfriend and also sleeping with her. He had been her lover for almost a year, after fifteen years of gay life.

Our conversation held the rapt attention of the other party guests under the patio tent. I had a feeling they were all straight. The shock potential was irresistible.

"What is the *strangest* thing to you about sex with men?" he asked me.

"I was totally unprepared for birth control," I said. All eyes settled on my belly. "No, I mean even before this!" I insisted. "What an awesome responsibility to consider every time you get turned on! I haven't connected sex to reproduction in years, and frankly, it's bizarre."

A couple underneath the umbrella left. It was probably the first time they'd ever heard themselves referred to as

140

some sort of puzzling phenomenon of the animal kingdom.

"I'd never been on a date before I met my baby's father," I said. "I was thirty years old and I had never in my life been out for a drink at a straight bar with a man."

Phillip nodded empathetically, so I went on. "The last time I had sex with men, we were demonstrating against Nixon by day, eating psychedelic mushrooms by night, and fucking in between. No one I knew went out on 'dates.' If you liked each other, you got it on. I had no feeling for contemporary heterosexual courtship."

Phillip broached the subject of sex itself. "Sex between men is more competitive," he contended, "because even if they both want to get fucked, there's a battle over who's going to submit first. With women, the tension is over pacing. Women want it slower; it takes them longer to get off, so that's where they exert pressure. With men, once the power balance is dealt with, coming doesn't take all that that long."

"That's true," I said, sucking my ice cubes hard. "With a man, I pretty much know where sex is heading. There's the big penis/vagina event, and then it's almost always over with his orgasm. With women, at least in the beginning, there's no such thing as foreplay. You have no idea how you're going to come, what kind of touching is going to be the climax, or how long sex will continue after you've had your first orgasm. My straight friend Jenny says that's why she could never do it with a girl—the anxiety of the unknown."

One of the umbrella people interrupted. "When are you expecting, Susie?"

"Any minute now," I said, reaching for my hat to block the sun. I had a button pinned to the straw that said *I got this way from kissing boys.*

"Did you get that at the gay day parade?" Phillip asked. But of course.

A year later, I had a baby girl, no boyfriend *or* girlfriend,

141

but a lot more thoughts on the subject. Most of my gay friends have had some sort of heterosexual experience. It was provocative to ask them—particularly the ones who had been gay for years—about the differences between men and women as lovers.

My friends Kitty and Marie, who form a sort of bulldagger quorum on any subject, worked themselves into quite a foam complaining that when it comes to taking a woman to bed, they had to do "all the work." They spoke about their needle-in-the-haystack search for a fem who could flip them and fuck them properly. By comparison, they remembered their straight experiences some twenty years ago as being non-orgasmic, but a real vacation. "You just let them do all the huffing and puffing," Kitty recalled.

My gay men friends, who were equally long in the tooth, also had scathing criticism to heap upon their male lovers, but their focus wasn't so much on what happened in bed as out of it. The egos! The attitudes as big as ozone holes! The neediness bordering on mania!

The way men and women dish each other falls neatly into gender blocks regardless of their sexual orientation. The stereotypical straight man's complaint about women is that they are too passive and reluctant in bed, while any five minute conversation with a straight woman will reveal her deep contempt for men's arrogance and infantile demands. The postscript is that these aggravations don't matter one whit when it comes to who desires whom.

One evening a year after we'd met, I got a call from Phillip. He no longer had a girlfriend, but he was writing a story for *Self* magazine, a novel excerpt in fact, about what it was like to be a gay man in a relationship with a woman.

I remembered that *Self* was chock full of self-analysis quizzes with multiple choice answers, designed to find out if you were an ambitious career girl or a dud in the sack. I could see Phillip's novel as a series of such questions:

"Ten Ways to Find Out If Your Boyfriend Is a Fag."

Phillip's story had raised so many eyebrows in the women's magazine kingdom that the Phil Donahue show had called him and was scheduling him for a program. They wanted a female counterpart to go along with this subject, and he'd thought of me.

"Do we get to give the nitty-gritty details," I asked, "as long as we don't say naughty words?"

"Of course!" Phillip was supremely confident. "That's what these shows thrive on, you know, titillating anecdotes. But you have to think up a whole bunch of responses to possible questions before the producer calls to pre-interview you."

"To make sure I'm not a nut?"

"Exactly."

I haven't spoken with a lot of television people, but I've read so much about them that I wasn't surprised by the gushing flattery they greet you with. What a horrible job they have, pretending that everyone is FASCINATING and that they'd give anything to be on your side. They even leave you their home phone numbers. You can call them at eleven o'clock at night and hear their kids screaming in the background, yet they still manage to put on the dog.

"We are so EXCITED about having you on this show, Susie!" It was Abby, the assistant producer. "Phillip says you're just WONDERFUL!"

I was ready to get down to business. "I'm not doing any 'God' shows," I told her. "I do not want to discuss Adam and Eve or Adam and Steve. I only want to talk about sex—the physical and emotional differences between sleeping with men and women."

"ABSOLUTELY!" Abby said, "That's why you're so PERFECT for this show!"

"The most obvious differences are physical," I continued, "but people rarely talk about all the less obvious consequences that come from the contrast in our bodies."

Abby stopped squealing and started taking dictation.

"I'm very tall," I told her, "and I have never been with a woman bigger than me. Most of the men I've been with are about my size, but they're stronger. With men, I can automatically assume that it's okay to roughhouse, that I can push them and grab them and slap them around, in fun or in foreplay. I don't worry about them getting hurt or frightened.

"With women, although plenty like to wrestle and play rough, you have to check it out one step at a time. Since I'm always the bigger one with women, I am more careful and gentle. It brings out protective feelings I don't have with men."

Abby murmured "Uh-huh," without exclamation points. Maybe this wasn't sexy enough for her.

"Then there are nipples," I said. "With a woman lover, one assumes she wants her breasts caressed and sucked, or admired. With most gay men, you'd assume the same thing. But the average straight man has to overcome feeling he's a pervert if he enjoys the attention I pay to his nipples. Having *any* sexual feelings in his breast makes him feel like a girl; he questions his masculine nature instead of just feeling normal."

"Oh, that's EXCELLENT!" Abby gasped. I was finally using the right grease.

"One last thing," she said, "I'm trying to find a COUPLE who've also had this experience, whether or not both of them are bisexual, to see how they resolve that issue in their relationship."

I was a little disappointed. I had hoped Phillip and I would hog the whole show to ourselves. "Most couples I know don't want to to talk about their sex lives on national TV," I said. "But I'll think about it."

I called Phillip up and asked him what he was going to wear.

New York was at its sweaty smelliest when we arrived. I

came with baby Aretha and her father Carter (now on speaking, but not fucking, terms) who was nanny-in-charge. The Donahue show picked us up in a limo at the airport, but the air conditioning was broken. It was rush hour.

Carter had tricked one of his old girlfriends into believing that *he* was invited onto Donahue to express his views on women. He showed me an eleven-page letter Jennifer had written to him begging him to reconsider. She thought the Donahue show had obviously asked him to appear because he would surely make an ass out of himself with his neo-chauvinist attitudes.

"She certainly understands the talk show mentality: exploit the ignorant," I said. I had come knowing that they had to have a trick up their sleeve for me. The only question was: How unnerving and humiliating would it be?

Phillip lives in New York, so he didn't have to do anything the next morning but brush his hair fifty times before the limo came to pick him up for the show. I wanted Carter and Aretha with me backstage, so I had major diaper bag preparations to distract me before the car came to collect us at the hotel. It was one of those long limousines, with two rows of leather seats facing each other. But it wasn't Phillip lounging in the back seat. It was a very blond pink-faced man and his female companion, who looked as flushed as he did, and very pregnant to boot.

This was the trick.

The couple didn't say a word. I introduced myself as if we might just be sharing a cab.

"Oh yes, we are guests on the show today too," said Raggedy Ann. "We've heard all about you." The snake was about to pop out of the can.

Raggedy Andy up. "My name is Jim, and this is my wife Anna. We are members of Exodus."

Say no more, buddy. Exodus is a well-publicized ministry that converts sinning homosexuals into God-fearing Christians.

"I didn't know Exodus was in New York," I said, looking down at my knees and wondering how they could be so close to rubbing a born-again fundamentalist's.

"Oh no, we're from Florida," the wife said. She looked a little unsteady.

"How far along are you?" I asked.

"This is the sixth month."

The last thing I would have done when I was six months pregnant would be to get hot and heavy on the Phil Donahue show. I looked over at her husband again. He seemed dressed carefully to look straight, but not so straight as to be unfashionable. A dark purple silk shirt, black tie, and wool pants. She was silky too, in pastels and gold jewelry.

The car was stifling. My thighs were glued with sweat to the seat. I could smell my cunt. The wife was on the verge of saying something.

"We're missionaries!" She finally perked up.

Unbelievable. Why was I being so polite? Just because we were fellow performers in a circus act? I wasn't sure Anna and Jim knew that yet.

At NBC studios, Abby came flying out to greet us, teeth flashing, hair bobbling.

"You didn't tell me about the Christian missionaries," I said.

"OH NO! REALLY?"

I knew a threat when I heard one, however effervescent. My bullshit decoder ring lit up, reading: "It is too late for you to back out now. You don't dare do anything to fuck up our show." The biggest trick of all had been leading me to believe that my appearance on this show would send viewers racing out to buy my book.

I heard the audience manager out in the live studio, practicing applause with the two hundred eager Donahue-ites, spreading adrenalin on them like mayonnaise. Phil Donahue himself approached the four of us waiting at the curtain. He was tall; he was a star; he told us to leave our table manners at home: blurt out, interrupt, say anything the moment it pops into our heads. For god's sake, don't sit there contemplating.

The green light came on—SHOWTIME! The audience roared. I walked on stage, and good ole Abby grabbed me by my shoulder.

"I forgot to tell you ONE thing," she said. "Don't talk about NIPPLES or ROUGH SEX—Phil doesn't like that."

PHIL DOESN'T LIKE NIPPLES? The studio audience screamed—somebody has a job to keep them screaming continuously. Up on stage were four little orange chairs attached to each other, too small for any grown-up. Wifey sat at one end, then her "no longer a homosexual" husband, then me, kissing-close to him, and finally Phillip.

We had our work cut out for us if we were going to get in a word about sex on this show. As much as I resented the born-agains' presence, they seemed as fragile as eggs— I was a little worried they might crack before the hour was up.

Anna kept talking about how she wanted to be obedient to the Lord, the Lord she knew "through Jesus Christ"— what does that mean? I felt like saying, "Oh, I know the Lord through Ralph Williams." Jim told the story of how he finally rejected a life of homosexual perversion to find the true light. During a commercial break he asked me if I had been molested as a child.

If I couldn't talk about rough nipples and stiff sex, then I was going to ask some hard questions of my own. I interrupted Donahue, who had been grabbing enough empty straws to fill a soda fountain.

"Anna, I want to ask you something." I looked in her innocent eyes. "Was there anything that attracted you to your husband because he was different from other straight men, because he came from a gay perspective?"

I had no idea what dynamite that would be. Anna's voice

cracked. "Jim is very sensitive and very artistic, but that has nothing to do with his former gay lifestyle, nothing at all!"

I turned to Phillip, my ally. "And you, does your girlfriend appreciate anything about you because you're gay?" I asked him.

He was ready. "Yes, she does, because just like a woman I know how it feels to be. . . *entered*, not only the physical part, but on an emotional level as well."

This time the audience screamed without any prompting. Half the women out there desperately wanted to fuck Phillip, and half the men wanted to kill him.

A young woman got up and addressed the next question to me. "Given your views on sexuality, how are you going to raise your child to deal with these issues?"

I went for it. "Well, you've noticed that for this entire show, we've been perfectly comfortable talking about personal issues like god and religion, but almost useless at discussing sex. I hope to give my daughter the kind of sex education I never had when I was a little girl. I hope she will meet and know people of all types of sexual orientations, so that when she grows up she won't fall to pieces or collapse in giggles whenever sex comes up."

Even my voice was starting to crack now. The show was almost over. I barely remember the last few comments, except from one geezer who got up and demanded that I stop knocking heterosexual intercourse and try it sometime. Buddy, I would have tried it right then if I could have gotten out of those baby torture seats. As the credits rolled, a pretty young woman got up and asked Philip and me if we had considered getting married. Hmm, he's not my type, even though we have a lot in common, knowing how it is to be "entered" and all.

No, I didn't say that. We didn't utter half of what we'd talked about before. Phillip's challenge—that once one is gay, one can't lose that perspective or feeling through subsequent heterosexual practice—is on the edge of queer theory, let alone the pages of *Self*. It used to be pretty simple: Homosexuality meant same sex-couplings. Now gay identity is up for grabs—from fag hags like Anna to celebrity dykes like me with baby and ex-boyfriend backstage.

A middle-aged Haitian woman with harlequin spectacles came up to me after the cameras went down, wanting a closer look.

She was a new immigrant; her English was not smooth. "How did you learn about sex, where do you go, a woman, to learn about sex?"

I was curious about her attraction to me, and I scribbled down a few referrals. But what a question she had asked! Where *do* we go? Why can't we talk about nipples and orgasms and genderfuck and why it's fun to wrestle on the floor—without prior censorship or approval? Phil Donahue doesn't have a clue, and I'm not waiting for my next invitation.

BLINDSEXUAL

The bisexual dream: a lover in perfect harmony with the duality of human nature; sensitive to male and female desires, basking in the sensuality of each sex.

That's what I believed when I first considered my bisexuality. I was sixteen; I had just been kissed, and in my case, it was a two-headed introduction. Sitting on the next-door neighbor's bed, I kissed my best girlfriend, and then, turning my head to the other side, I kissed him. Then all three of us made love. I was so pleased with myself you'd have thought I'd just baked two perfect cherry pies.

My first time was very much in sync with my political ideals. I thought that if everyone would get into a big waterbed, smoke a joint, and rub noses, we could live in peace, tranquillity and a perpetual state of arousal—my solution to world strife. This was before I had my own nose rubbed in that jealous, selfish pot of piss called human nature.

I came out as bi before there was a "bisexual movement" as such, before the B-word was attached to the Lesbian and Gay Freedom Day parades, community centers, and racquetball clubs. When I was sixteen, I would have gleefully joined them all and been pleased to find a political program that matched my bedroom behavior.

You've heard what the bisexual movement has to say about "bi-phobia." Behavioral scientists know that human sexuality spans a spectrum from very homo to very hetero, and most folks fall down some weird crack in the middle. Accused of being "infantile," or "fence-sitters," described as "traitors" by the gay world and "perverts" by the straight one, bisexual activists have told the status quo on both sides of the argument to grow up and get real.

Fifteen years after my coming out, when the banners started waving for bisexual recognition, I nodded my head in robot-like agreement with the ten- and twelve-point programs, but I didn't join up. You didn't see me in the contingent; I wasn't on the float. The bisexual movement, as such, leaves me cold, as does much of the political gay movement it comes from. How can this be?

When I first proclaimed my bisexuality in the early seventies, I was very intimidated by my lesbian elders who pointed a blunt finger at my transgressions, damning me to the Judas seat of heterosexual privilege. I hadn't even had the "privilege" of having a relationship with anyone yet, and I had only had sex a dozen times. Yet I was loyal to the principles of feminism and gay liberation. It tore me apart to think that I would ever do anything to hurt our cause, in or out of bed.

I look at my sexual history today and see that my relationships have more often than not been with people who were secretly attracted to my bisexuality rather than repulsed by it. Some of them were leaders and some of them were led by me. I was intimate with people who wanted understanding for their capacity to love more than one person at the same time. I was cherished by men who desired other men and who desired their own womanliness. I was treasured by women who valued my appeal to men, because those were the same qualities that moved them as gay women. My lovers have been butches, perverts, bohemians, philanderers and Johnny-come-latently bisexuals themselves.

I used to get in a tizzy because I wanted a written proclamation from gay society saying that bisexuals—in fact, all sexual deviants—were welcome and considered family. I even wrote a platform statement expressing those sentiments for a gay convention, held in 1980 to fight the Moral Majority. I was all but thrown bodily out of the room.

Guess what? No one gets a proclamation. If you want to be in the gay life, then you sit your ass down in the middle of it, and you don't just get up and move because someone doesn't like you. Gay life isn't a cherry pie; it's a fire walk.

The political urge to wed gay rights to the rights of sexual minorities in a genuine sexual liberation movement has made for strange bedfellows. It's straightforward enough to ask for an end to prejudice. It's preposterous to ask sexual beings to stuff ourselves into the rapidly imploding social categories of straight or gay or bi, as if we could plot our sexual behavior on a conscientious, predictable curve.

A true sexual liberation movement does not simply deal with pride. Sexual liberation challenges our hearts with unbearable feelings that no one is proud of: jealousy, sexual shame, and the uncontrollable attraction to risk. Bisexuality adds a brutal twist to these subjects only because it confronts all the prejudices between and among men and women.

Don't talk to me about gay pride or bi pride. Love has no pride—that's the banner the real world marches under. When I was young, I was very hurt by political ringmasters who said they wouldn't talk, fuck or work with me because I was bisexual. Now that I've worked, fucked and talked with them *all*, I'm not hurt anymore, because I know their secret. They desire what they condemn.

The first time I spoke to a group about my bisexuality was in 1978 in a Cal State/Long Beach class called "The Lesbian." My hands shook as I addressed the circle of twenty young women. The Cal State Marching Band played "America the Beautiful" on the quad just outside our door.

No one said anything after I finished my speech. Finally, the most articulate student in class, "The Lesbian" to end all lesbians, a redheaded grad student with peerless feminist credentials, raised her eyebrow, and delivered my death sentence:

"How do you justify giving wimmin's energy and lesbian knowledge to our oppressors," she asked, "and then expect any principled lesbian-identified woman to trust you?"

I stared at her like a rabbit caught in the middle of the road. I did not know the answer to that question. Tears came to my eyes. I didn't expect anyone to trust or love me. My sexual confidence was all on paper. I had only been to bed with plain old ᵗeenage girls, who probably thought I was the only principled lesbian feminist between us. When we made love, my mouth was full of their honey, wet from their lips and their cunts. The world of our affection and romance seemed very distant from this fluorescent-lit inquisition.

I could not have predicted at the time that one day I would be a lesbian sex expert and that this very same redhead would be living with her husband and two kids in a suburb outside of Chicago. My politics at the time did not allow for the most important principle of all: *Shit happens*.

As wounded as I was by gay accusations, I was sensitive myself to the daily grind of heterosexual arrogance. I never liked to tell people that I was bi. Straight men took it as a come-on line, an advertisement. Better that they should have seen my dyke button a mile away. Dykes took it as an indication that I was playing games. Wrong again. Latent lesbian girls took my bisexual admission as some sort of invitation to them to rag on about how repulsive *real* man-hating lesbians were. "Oh, I'm sorry," I wanted to say. "You misunderstand me. I'm a man-hating bisexual."

But I didn't say that. I told all but the most sincere that I was gay. It hardly seemed to matter. For ten years, my live-action sexual encounters with men were few, far between, and rather odd. One time, I fucked the Christmas UPS man who made deliveries at my boring job. Another time, I spent the night with one of my childhood political heroes, an old man of sixty-eight who once led a waterfront strike and now has diabetes. He couldn't get an erection and felt very badly about it.

"It doesn't matter," I told him. "I'm a lesbian, I don't expect it . . . . I just want to be with you." His intimacy was a privilege for me.

I understand now that a mouthful like "heterosexual privilege" doesn't have anything to do with the luxury or honor of bedding down with my oppressor—or my mentor. It's just an academic way to describe the flat-out devastation of losing your woman to a man. I've played every humiliating soap opera scene in that book. I've woken up next to women who couldn't look me in the eye after clinging to me all night, and I've watched them run to their boy friends so fast they tripped over their shoelaces.

One memorable evening at a very drunken party, I watched my lover, Sherry, disappear behind a bedroom door with one of my roommates, a big blond man a foot taller than me. I pressed my ear against the door and blocked out the B-52s album blaring in the background. I heard him humping her. I couldn't believe it. *Why don't you dance with me?* I was so shocked that I was bold enough to open the door and walk in. "Sherry?" I called out to the long hair trailing over the bed. Her tiny body was covered by his. I was so close to them, it was remarkable they didn't notice me at all. I finally left them, closed the door, and resolved to wait there, all night if necessary, to confront her when she walked out.

At four A.M., some fresh arrivals rolled in the front door with a new keg. "Hey, your girlfriend just jumped out the bedroom window," one of them said to me. "What's her problem?"

I ran outside, but the only bit of Sherry I found was the soft spot in the grass where she'd landed. *Everybody goes to parties, they dance this mess around. . . .*

Nowadays Sherry is a butch working on the Manhattan stock exchange, and she has lived with the same woman for ten years. But that was one bad night.

I need to find the redhead, "The Lesbian," and tell her this story. Sherry betrayed *me*, not homosexuality, not the lesbian empire. She spread her legs for that man; I stood motionless and watched them; she flew out the window; I cried, and then we started all over again. We are capable of every betrayal and every forgiveness that follows.

I pick up my bible, Roland Barthes' *A Lover's Discourse*, or "Lovers Disco," as I call it. "The sentiment of amorous suffering explodes in this cry: 'I can't go on. . . .' "

But you do. "Nothing works out, but it keeps going on."

I did not imagine I could go on after Sherry left me. Losing a woman to a man is as close to the burning sensation of childhood ridicule as one can experience. You feel incompetent, unable to compete, yet it makes you sick to even think of comparing yourself with that . . . *thing*. Not even that *thing* between his legs, but that thing between his ears that makes every man think that he's God.

When I left my girlfriend because I fell for a man, the harshest thing she said to me was an accusation thrown at my back, screamed as I climbed up the hill to my car filled with my half of the household furnishings.

"Have you fucked your boyfriend yet?" A direct hit.

Yes, I had fucked him, and I would do it again and again. I wanted to scream at her, "You don't understand, you'll never understand."

Had she never been engulfed with desire so extreme as to spit in the face of all her principles, beliefs, morals? Of course she had. She was twelve years older than me. She understood, but I didn't.

To submit to lust is to declare a panic, a state of body emergency. My shame at leaving my girlfriend, who had fucked me in the ass with her arm, who had tasted every fluid in my body, who had brought me to the brink again and again and loved me so well—how could I do this to her?

Just watch me—and then watch yourself follow in my footsteps, the steps that lead so faithfully into every dark alley we take such pains to shun. I did not want to be straight. I had been content with my bisexuality only as long as men were tangential to it. When I fucked this man, it was an act of greatest perversion.

In my shame I picked up "Lovers Disco" once again and sat down on the toilet:

"I am reduced to endurance. . . . I suffer without adjustment, I persist without intensity, always bewildered, never discouraged. I am a Daruma doll, a legless toy endlessly poked and pushed, but finally regaining its balance, assured by an inner balancing pin.

"But WHAT is my balancing pin? The force of love?

". . . Such is life, falling over seven times and getting up eight."

Intellectually, we always favor those of our own sex, even if they're not our sexual partners. Bisexuals are the same as everyone else in this regard; we just get more opportunity to view the spectacle. To be with the opposite sex is never "better"; it's a classic compromise, however compelling. Some think that it is "feminism" for women to prefer women and "chauvinism" for men to prefer men. But the prejudice is older than that. You are always a little disdainful of your opposite. I am capable of believing in love, certainly lust, but never in equality between the sexes.

Jealousy, however, is the great equalizer. Security and exclusivity—promises broken as often as they are offered—are high on every lover's list of demands. I despise jealousy. I control it only with discipline; it is like a skin I cannot shed.

I search for the lovers who won't consider my bisexuality a *de facto* threat, who will not fear that to love me is to be in perpetual competition with their sex. That fear is the true reaction to bisexuality, not political epithets. Accusing a bisexual of being a traitor reveals one's desperate, and quite human, fear of rejection. I can barely accept that feature in myself.

Let me be honest with you, and let me be shameful, as it seems so essential to my discipline: I don't want to hear that *you're* "bisexual" either, especially just after you've fucked me blind. Don't tell me who you "are." I'm a mere mortal, jealous and vulnerable, and I might fall for you in a big way. Show me what you can do. If you succeed in blinding me, I will follow you, potentially into loss, betrayal, into the fire walk. It will be personal; it will not necessarily be principled. In the moment after orgasm, this is what is memorable. And for many moments after.

Books from Cleis Press

Sexuality/Lesbian Studies

A Lesbian Love Advisor by Celeste West. ISBN: 0-939416-27-1 24.95 cloth;
ISBN: 0-939416-26-3 9.95 paper.

Boomer: Railroad Memoirs by Linda Niemann. ISBN: 0-939416-55-7
12.95 paper.

Different Daughters: A Book by Mothers of Lesbians edited by Louise
Rafkin. ISBN: 0-939416-12-3 21.95 cloth; ISBN: 0-939416-13-1 9.95 paper.

Different Mothers: Sons & Daughters of Lesbians Talk About Their Lives
edited by Louise Rafkin. ISBN: 0-939416-40-9 24.95 cloth;
ISBN: 0-939416-41-7 9.95 paper.

Good Sex: Real Stories From Real People by Julia Hutton.
ISBN: 0-939416-56-5 24.95 cloth; ISBN: 0-939416-57-3 12.95 paper.

Long Way Home: The Odyssey of a Lesbian Mother and Her Children by
Jeanne Jullion. ISBN: 0-939416-05-0 8.95 paper.

More Serious Pleasure: Lesbian Erotic Stories and Poetry edited by the
Sheba Collective. ISBN: 0-939416-48-4 24.95 cloth; ISBN: 0-939416-47-6
9.95 paper.

Queer & Pleasant Danger: Writing Out My Life by Louise Rafkin.
ISBN: 0-939416-60-3 24.95 cloth; ISBN: 0-939416-61-1 9.95 paper.

Serious Pleasure: Lesbian Erotic Stories and Poetry edited by the Sheba
Collective. ISBN: 0-939416-46-8 24.95 cloth; ISBN: 0-939416-45-X
9.95 paper.

Sex Work: Writings by Women in the Sex Industry edited by Frédérique
Delacoste and Priscilla Alexander. ISBN: 0-939416-10-7 24.95 cloth;
ISBN: 0-939416-11-5 16.95 paper.

Susie Bright's Sexual Reality: A Virtual Sex World Reader.
ISBN: 0-939416-58-1 24.95 cloth; ISBN: 0-939416-59-X 9.95 paper

Susie Sexpert's Lesbian Sex World by Susie Bright. ISBN: 0-939416-34-4
24.95 cloth; ISBN: 0-939416-35-2 9.95 paper.

Fiction

Another Love by Erzsébet Galgóczi. ISBN: 0-939416-52-2 24.95 cloth;
ISBN: 0-939416-51-4 8.95 paper.

Cosmopolis: Urban Stories by Women edited by Ines Rieder.
ISBN: 0-939416-36-0 24.95 cloth; ISBN: 0-939416-37-9 9.95 paper.

Night Train To Mother by Ronit Lentin. ISBN: 0-939416-29-8 24.95 cloth;
ISBN: 0-939416-28-X 9.95 paper.

The One You Call Sister: New Women's Fiction edited by Paula Martinac.
ISBN: 0-939416-30-1 24.95 cloth; ISBN: 0-939416031-X 9.95 paper.

Unholy Alliances: New Women's Fiction edited by Louise Rafkin.
ISBN: 0-939416-14-X 21.95 cloth; ISBN: 0-939416-15-8 9.95 paper.

The Wall by Marlen Haushofer. ISBN: 0-939416-53-0 24.95 cloth;
ISBN: 0-939416-54-9 9.95 paper.

Latin American Studies

Beyond the Border: A New Age in Latin American Women's Fiction edited
by Nora Erro-Peralta and Caridad Silva-Núñez. ISBN: 0-939416-42-5 24.95
cloth; ISBN: 0-939416-43-3 12.95 paper.

The Little School: Tales of Disappearance and Survival in Argentina by
Alicia Partnoy. ISBN: 0-939416-08-5 21.95 cloth; ISBN: 0-939416-07-7
9.95 paper.

Revenge of the Apple by Alicia Partnoy. ISBN: 0-939416-62-X 24.95 cloth;
ISBN: 0-939416-63-8 8.95 paper.

You Can't Drown the Fire: Latin American Women Writing in Exile edited
by Alicia Partnoy. ISBN: 0-939416-16-6 24.95 cloth; ISBN: 0-939416-17-4
9.95 paper.

Health/Recovery Titles:

The Absence of the Dead Is Their Way of Appearing by Mary Winfrey
Trautmann. ISBN: 0-939416-04-2 8.95 paper.

AIDS: The Women edited by Ines Rieder and Patricia Ruppelt.
ISBN: 0-939416-20-4 24.95 cloth; ISBN: 0-939416-21-2 9.95 paper

Don't: A Woman's Word by Elly Danica. ISBN: 0-939416-23-9 21.95 cloth;
ISBN: 0-939416-22-0 8.95 paper

1 in 3: Women with Cancer Confront an Epidemic edited by Judith Brady.
ISBN: 0-939416-50-6 24.95 cloth; ISBN: 0-939416-49-2 10.95 paper.

Voices in the Night: Women Speaking About Incest edited by Toni A.H.
McNaron and Yarrow Morgan. ISBN: 0-939416-02-6 9.95 paper.

With the Power of Each Breath: A Disabled Women's Anthology edited by
Susan Browne, Debra Connors and Nanci Stern. ISBN: 0-939416-09-3 24.95
cloth; ISBN: 0-939416-06-9 10.95 paper.

Woman-Centered Pregnancy and Birth by the Federation of Feminist
Women's Health Centers. ISBN: 0-939416-03-4 11.95 paper.

Women's Studies

Peggy Deery: An Irish Family at War by Nell McCafferty.
ISBN: 0-939416-38-7 24.95 cloth; ISBN: 0-939416-39-5 9.95 paper.

The Shape of Red: Insider/Outsider Reflections by Ruth Hubbard and
Margaret Randall. ISBN: 0-939416-19-0 24.95 cloth; ISBN: 0-939416-18-2
9.95 paper.

Women & Honor: Some Notes on Lying by Adrienne Rich.
ISBN: 0-939416-44-1 3.95 paper.

Animal Rights

And a Deer's Ear, Eagle's Song and Bear's Grace: Relationships Between Animals and Women edited by Theresa Corrigan and Stephanie T. Hoppe. ISBN: 0-939416-38-7 24.95 cloth; ISBN: 0-939416-39-5 9.95 paper.

With a Fly's Eye, Whale's Wit and Woman's Heart: Relationships Between Animals and Women edited by Theresa Corrigan and Stephanie T. Hoppe. ISBN: 0-939416-24-7 24.95 cloth; ISBN: 0-939416-25-5 9.95 paper.

Since 1980, Cleis Press has published progressive books by women. We welcome your order and will ship your books as quickly as possible. Individual orders must be prepaid (U.S. dollars only). Please add 15% shipping. PA residents add 6% sales tax. Mail orders: Cleis Press, PO Box 8933, Pittsburgh PA 15221. MasterCard and Visa orders: $25 minimum—include account number, exp. date, and signature. FAX your credit card order: (412) 937-1567. Or, phone us Mon-Fri, 9 am - 5 pm EST: (412) 937-1555.